Made in America

The Business of Apparel and Sewn Products Manufacturing

Sue Pekarsky Gary and Connie Ulasewicz

Third Edition

MADE IN AMERICA: THE BUSINESS OF APPAREL & SEWN PRODUCTS MANUFACTURING

PLEASE READ:

THE NAME GarmentoSpeak® IS A PLAY ON WORDS. IN THE PAST, THE TERM GARMENTO DEFINITELY HAD A NEGATIVE SPIN TO IT. YET, A GARMENTO SPOKE THE LANGUAGE OF THE INDUSTRY. TODAY GarmentoSpeak® POSITIVELY PROVIDES YOU WITH THE LANGUAGE AND SKILLS YOU NEED, AS YOU TURN YOUR DESIGN IDEAS INTO PROFIT AS PART OF THE GARMENT INDUSTRY.

WE HAVE DONE OUR VERY BEST TO GIVE YOU USEFUL AND ACCURATE INFORMATION IN THIS BOOK, BUT WE CANNOT GUARANTEE THAT THE INFORMATION WILL BE APPROPRIATE TO YOUR PARTICULAR SITUATION. IT IS YOUR RESPONSIBILITY TO VERIFY ALL INFORMATION AND ALL LAWS DISCUSSED IN THIS BOOK BEFORE RELYING ON THEM. IN ALL SITUATIONS INVOLVING LOCAL, STATE OR FEDERAL LAW, OBTAIN SPECIFIC INFORMATION FROM THE APPROPRIATE GOVERNMENT AGENCY OR A COMPETENT PERSON.

Cover design by Lisa Louie, Ideal Solutions Graphic Design.

Published by GarmentoSpeak®
   1380 Tilton Road
   Sebastopol, CA 95472-9110
   P 707-823-4001
   F 707-823-5772
   www.garmentospeak.com
   garmento@garmentospeak.com

Library of Congress Catalog Card Number 2001117890

ISBN 0-9662009-3-4
Printed and bound in the United States of America.
10 9 8 7 6 5 4 3 2 1

Contents

FOREWORD

Ask anyone buried in it up to their eyeballs—apparel manufacturing is unlike any other business venture. The development and manufacturing processes are complicated and rarely the same twice. Production techniques are labor-intensive and time-sensitive. The industry language can be imprecise, if not downright confusing. Terms of business relationships are measured in the briefest of timelines, usually season to season. Profits can be swallowed up with just the slightest miscalculation. The days are long and filled with anxiety and challenges. Welcome to our world!

So, if it's so darned hard, why are so many talented entrepreneurs devoting their life's blood to this endeavor? Because it's fun, challenging, glamorous, right-brained, left-brained, all-consuming, fast-paced, creative and fulfilling on a hundred different levels. In short, owning your own apparel design and manufacturing company is addicting to the soul.

If you have taken the time to find and purchase *Made in America*, congratulations. You are already well on the way to a place few have visited so early in the game.

My respected colleagues Sue Pekarsky Gary and Connie Ulasewicz have combined their knowledge and experiences in this book. An important reference work, it contains all that a would-be apparel designer/manufacturer needs to know before actually committing to this wild and crazy life. Within these pages you will find invaluable business advice. Read the book carefully and read it again. Keep *Made in America* handy, because I guarantee that you will be referring to it for many years to come.

Welcome to the apparel and sewn products business!

Randall Harris
Executive Director
San Francisco Fashion Industries

INTRODUCTION

Designs and creativity drive the fashion and textile entrepreneur to produce a wearable, usable, salable expression of initial ideas. The business itself is down and dirty, and one's product is in constant peril of either appearing passé or being "knocked off"—copied. Consequently, in writing our book, we know we are speaking to creative people. You need every bit of relevant information we can give you so that you can operate competitively in the arenas of garment, textile, sewn products and home furnishings design and manufacture.

Our experience is as designers and artists for over thirty years, garment manufacturers for a total of twelve years and garment industry consultants and teachers of fashion studies curricula at California colleges for a total of twelve years. We have successfully turned our fashion design ideas into profitable ventures in the rag business. As teachers, writers and consultants we have been effectively imparting information for many years by offering popular courses and seminars.

This book presents how-to material geared to all you creative people—a population most worthy of making money from your ideas. This concise handbook provides easy access to an excellent overview of the business—no matter in which part of the country or world you live.

Positive reception of your design ideas has caused you to consider producing or manufacturing them for a greater exposure in and share of the market place. The design—your design—is the driving force behind your consideration of manufacturing as a means to recognition and financial success. Design-based manufacturing is the term we use to identify production in quantity of a product that you have designed.

Designing may come easily to you. It is also satisfying to create and then to receive positive feedback on your creations. But, taking the leap to being a manufacturer brings you instantly into the demands of "doing business"—another world. Also, your creativity will need to respond to maintaining a company image or look. At the same time, you must have something new each season. Staying *au courant* and fashion-forward is as important as maintaining a consistent look or image. Suddenly there will be limits to and demands on your creative endeavors. Fitting your ideas to your company's needs may sometimes be an exhilarating experience and sometimes discouraging.

Entrepreneurship is currently a popular identity. It is an answer to being at the mercies of the job market, downsizing and loss of benefits. Being your own boss, your own person, is appealing to many of us who have lots of ideas, drive and focus. The lure of being captain of the ship or commander of the fleet needs the balancing realities of being head of the company. For all the glory of being at the helm, there are the responsibilities of being in charge of a viable operation. For all the freedom to do what you want, there are the constraints of doing what is necessary to successfully stay in business.

In addition to being clever and in control, you must be organized and flexible. You need to be able to do many tasks and delegate responsibilities as necessary. You need to be goal-directed and to identify all the little steps to the goal, to see the big picture and to pay attention to details. In design-based garment, textile or associated industries and in craft manufacturing you will wear many hats. On any one day you may be designer, marketing director, sales manager, production manager, chief financial officer, quality control inspector *and* shipping clerk. You may use a variety of sales venues such as "brick and mortar" stores, catalogs, e-commerce and trade shows. If you find this daily variety appealing, then entrepreneurship as a design-based manufacturer is definitely something for you to consider.

ACKNOWLEDGMENTS

Many thanks to Barbara Brandt, Mary Lou Lange and Mary Ellen Ross for their time, invaluable suggestions and comments; to copy editor Carol Bee for her professional finesse; and to proofreader Phyllis Greene for her exacting eye. We also thank our patient family members—Mike, Katrina and Adam Lee and David Gary—we appreciate your support, understanding and love. We could not have completed this book without all of you.

CHAPTER 1: EVALUATING YOUR SKILLS AND PRODUCT FOR DEVELOPMENT

Some of you who are using this book are evaluating a product idea that you have already developed. You may even have sold a few. Suddenly you find yourself realizing, … "Wow, I need to figure out what I should have done." Some of you may be at the idea stage and are wondering how to find out if your idea is a viable one—can this design be produced and sold at a profit to an adequate market? For all of you, spending about ten to fifteen hours to go through this section will provide you with the information and answers you need to make a decision. Proceeding through the evaluation process and gathering information will help you clarify your thoughts and focus on the directions you should take to proceed with product development. Sometime, you will arrive at no—not necessarily what you want to hear. But pay attention to the results of all the research and decision making you do.

We show you how to gain the necessary insight into the value and marketability of your product and thus be able to operate from the position of strength that this knowledge creates for you. If you are not satisfied with your answers or you need additional help in sorting out some grey areas, then it is time to call a consultant to guide you through the process and help you gather the additional information you need to evaluate your design/product. Such a professional will cost hundreds to thousands of dollars.

Whether you sell or license your design idea or you decide to personally control its production and distribution you'll need information and careful preparation. Many designers want to just design and have someone else do everything else. Unfortunately, manufacturers looking for freelance designs to produce are few and far between. Therefore, it is important to evaluate your product and what is involved in producing it.

Hold These Thoughts...
•Honesty

•Energy

•Curiosity

Your "Manufacturer" Quotient

• **Sell/License**

1. Do you want to sell your design(s) to someone for a flat fee?   **Yes / No**

2. Do you want to license your design(s) to a manufacturer?   **Yes / No**

You need to decide to what degree you want to be involved in manufacturing your design/ product. If you are considering selling your design to someone else, you must understand that you will lose all rights to royalties, patents and/or copyrights and future profits. If you license your designs, you will retain ownership of the design, patents and/or copyrights and receive royalties from any sales of your design. Initially, you will receive some payment, as stipulated by the contract. Your first royalty payments will be reduced by the amount of this payment. The amount of royalty paid is on a sliding scale; the percentage of royalties increases as sales volume increases. Payment will be quarterly. You should retain the right to monitor their books to ensure that you are paid the correct amount of royalties.

• **Do It Yourself**

3. Do you want to manufacture your own designs?   **Yes / No**

You can manufacture/produce your designs either in-house in your own factory or by out-sourcing/contracting out the work to others. A **manufacturer** is a company/person who designs product, controls all or parts of production and sells directly to retailers. A manufacturer can have in-house production workers, be a contractor by performing work for other manufacturers or contract out all labor to a contractor. A **contractor** is a company/person who performs work on a large scale according to a contractual agreement, at a predetermined price.

To manufacture in-house you must evaluate your facilities for storage of materials, production equipment (cutting tables and sewing machines) and personnel to use this equipment. Additionally, you must consider the costs of buying or leasing equipment. If you hire employees, you will have a payroll: pay payroll taxes, insurances and benefits; and need to lease/buy equipment to make your design/product. Your **overhead costs** for employees, facilities, rent and utilities and so on are part of the **total cost** of producing your goods in-house. Your **direct labor costs** per piece will be less than the **piece price** that a contractor charges you. The contractor's piece price includes his overhead and profit. Either way, you need to know how much it is going to cost to make one of your design/product and where to find sources for at least materials.

Your Skills

- **Capitalize on Your Skills!**

Take an inventory of all your skills and see which ones you can use to make producing your design idea a reality. Below is a list of skills that may be useful to you. And you probably have skills you can apply to the success of your venture.

- **Design and Sewing Experience**

These hands-on skills or experiences directly relate to garment design and production. You may have previously acquired these skills or gained experience using them. You can easily translate the knowledge you already have to textile, apparel and sewn product design and manufacturing.

- Art or design training
- Artistic talent
- Pattern drafting skills

- Design skills
- Sewing skills
- Production sewing experience

- **General Business Experience**

Although experience in these areas may have been obtained in other businesses or professions, it is all applicable to the business of manufacturing textiles, apparel and sewn products.

- Sales and/or marketing experience
- Garment production experience
- Previous ownership of a small business
- Teaching experience
- Production experience in any field

- Managerial experience
- Ability to see the big picture
- People skills
- Public relations experience
- Attention to detail

Your Personal Availability and Commitment to This Design Idea

There are some essential questions you must answer—for yourself—in order to mentally prepare for evaluating your product. The following **personal inventory** addresses those areas of your life and business that are directly connected to and affected by being in business with a product of your own design. Most of these are short answers—yes or no; more space is supplied for longer answers.

As you go through the following questions, take the time to be thorough in your thought process. Explore the possibilities and ramifications. These questions focus first on you personally—your talents, motivation, personality and health. Next, explore your design ideas/product, the marketplace and rigors of manufacturing. If you do not have a clear answer, do the research necessary to get the information you need. Checking online, taking a look in a phone book or directory and making a few phone calls, checking out comparable goods in stores, having some clear talks with a knowledgeable friend or advisor, and thinking rationally are all ways to help you find the answers you need. Save the fantasies for designing and creating.

• Motivation

4. Is this design idea driving you toward expression and completion?   **Yes / No**

5. Are you driven by the desire to make money with your ideas?   **Yes / No**

6. Is your style to stick it out to the end, bitter or not?   **Yes / No**

7. Will others be personally involved with this project?   **Yes / No**

8. Do you know that you can work well with them?   **Yes / No**

9. Is this idea/project a learning process to some degree? In what areas? On what levels?

Yes/ No

Be as clear with yourself as you can on these points. Why *do* you want to start this business? Are you seeking creative satisfaction and strokes? Is making money the most important reason for your going into business? Understanding what is driving you to be a design-based manufacturer will allow you to focus your goals for your business plan and as your business develops.

- **Personality**

10. Do you want to be an entrepreneur?   **Yes / No**
11. Do you have the mental space to be designer, production manager, sales manager and accountant?   **Yes / No**
12. Can you grow with the business?   **Yes / No**

On any given day you will perform many different functions and wear many different hats. Often you will be shifting gears on a moment's notice and you must be flexible enough to jump right into your next operation.

13. Can you cope with the day-to-day stress of running a business?   **Yes / No**
14. Are you reliable?   **Yes / No**
15. Can you see the big picture?   **Yes / No**
16. Are you analytical?   **Yes / No**
17. Do you have the self-confidence to be a leader?   **Yes / No**
18. Can your ego take "Not interested," as well as "We love it"?   **Yes / No**

Customers and employees will be counting on you to be there and to perform. As we discussed earlier, being a businessperson requires a different mindset and outlook than being a designer. Are you/can you be both people? Success requires yes answers to questions 10 through18.

- **Time**

19. How much time can you devote to this project? Do you have children, family, friends to consider in the equation?
20. Do you currently work full-time?   **Yes / No**

As a business owner you will have the good fortune to work longer hours than you ever have before. Be prepared. The responsibility of making your dream come true is now yours.

21. Will you be able to devote time during regular business hours to this project? **Yes / No**

In order to buy your materials, work with contractors or employees and communicate with and be available to your customers, you must be available to do business with customers and suppliers during regular business hours. If you have infants or small children, it is essential that you have time to talk on the phone with no screaming children in the background. You can juggle many parts of a complex lifestyle, but doing business properly requires that you operate in a timely and appropriate manner. You cannot expect a customer to hold while you soothe a tearful child. You have flexibility being your own boss; use it in your own and your company's best interests.

- **Money**

22. Do you have money of your own with which to start your business? **Yes / No**
23. Will you be funding your garment business out-of-pocket as you go along? **Yes / No**
24. Can you borrow money? Family? Friends? A business loan? Other sources? **Yes / No**
25. Do you have collateral to get a personal loan? **Yes / No**
26. Are you aware of the need to write a business plan to get a loan from banks and other commercial lenders? **Yes / No**

You can start your business on a shoestring or do it out-of-pocket as you go along. Personal loans or lines of credit from your bank or credit cards are other options to get you started. As a rule, it is somewhere between impossible and impossibly difficult to get a commercial loan until you have been in business for at least two years. Some lending institutions do have loan programs for women and minorities starting a business. Check with your local SCORE office, part of the federal government's Small Business Administration, for local sources of these loans.

...and I thought only bowties were unattractive!!

Basic **start-up costs** include, but are not limited to the following:

Office Equipment

Telephone

Computer with modem for fax/email

Desk

Chairs

Filing cabinet

Licenses: Business, resale, etc.

Permits

Possible Rental of Office Space

Product Development

Pattern-making—the cost to develop a pattern for your design.

Fabric samples—the costs of the fabric that you use to make your samples.

Sample-making—the cost of actually producing the sample.

- **Health**

27. Do you have the health and vigor to run your own business?   **Yes / No**

You will need both! Suddenly, ten- or twelve-hour workdays and six- or seven-day workweeks will become the norm for you. There is so much to do, and in the beginning you will do most of it yourself. Because this business is most likely the making and selling of your design, you want it done right. You will be the watchdog who makes sure everything is done to your specs, or else!

Your business will be all-consuming in its early stages. Sometimes you will be driven to work those long hours and sometimes your business will demand it. You do not call in to take a sick day; you work around ill health as best you can. The show goes on! And, of course, you want enough energy left over to be a functional social being, not a zombie.

- **Space**

28. Do you have the physical space to design, produce and ship your goods?   **Yes / No**

29. Do you have space to grow—for physical operation of the business?   **Yes / No**

In some states—California, Hawaii, Indiana, Maryland, Massachusetts, Michigan, Missouri, New Jersey, New York and Ohio—there are laws prohibiting or controlling garment and accessory manufacturing in the home. These laws vary from strict and broad to minimal and easy to comply with. There are also local zoning laws to consider if you are initially planning to operate in your home or in a residential neighborhood. You may start your business on the dining room table, as many people have. This certainly maximizes existing space and eliminates renting or buying space. But if you plan to take an IRS deduction for an office/workplace in the home, you must adhere to all local, state and federal laws relative to home offices and to being a garment manufacturer; you must operate in a legally designated business space.

Remember to allow storage space for the raw materials that you will need to stockpile, and also for finished inventory, both of which need to be kept clean, unfaded, wrinkle-free and looking new.

- **Production Options**

30. Do you plan to make one-of-a-kind? Mass produce? Somewhere in between? **Yes / No**

31. Can you obtain your raw materials—fabric and trim, basically—in the (small) quantities you will need, at wholesale prices?   **Yes / No**

32. Can you easily and locally manufacture or have manufactured your design idea?

                                                                                  Yes / No

33. If your production will not be done locally, will you be able to easily maintain control of the manufacturing process to ensure quality and timely delivery?   **Yes / No**

- **Contacts and Resources**

34. Do you know people who can help you in various ways? People in the business? Other designers?   **Yes / No**

35. Are you able to conduct the research to find the people you will need to work for and with you?

                                                                                  Yes / No

How important to you is an already established network of professionals—designers, graders, pattern-makers, bookkeepers, accountants, graphic artists, printers, insurance agents, and so on—at the beginning of your venture? You can start this business with these contacts in place or you can develop them as you proceed. If you have already shopped around for these people you will be ready to make use of their services when you need them. You will feel secure if you know where to go for what you need and how much it is going to cost you. You probably have more usable contacts and resources than you realize. Your friends might be valuable contacts and resources also; be respectful of their time.

Review your answers to these questions. Are any clear patterns emerging? Is the direction you need to take obvious to you now? Will some things be smooth sailing and others require a great deal of work? Do the results of this survey and your ideas about developing your product mesh nicely? These personal issues are as important as any other part of developing your product. If you are not comfortable with the process, you need to resolve any problem issues by analyzing them. Then you can find solutions.

Your Product in the Marketplace

"Tools" You Will Need

- Phone
- Calculator
- Access to stores that sell similar products
- Access to the Internet
- Access to a (business) library
- Local yellow pages and those for the nearest big city (check your local library)

THE DISCOVERY OF ILLUSION DRESSING

©1994 CHAS ADDON

"Why, Zog, you look ten pounds slimmer!"

- **Market Research**

36. What are the demographics of your ideal customer? List findings and sources.

Age _____

Sex _____

Marital status _____

Occupation _____

Geographic location _____

Other _____

_____

In the orderly, objective process of gathering and evaluating information about your potential customers, it is essential that you analyze your market before you develop your product/product line. You want to manufacture a product that fits into or can create its own market niche. Remember to note the source of your information: website, librarian, bookstore clerk, etc., for future research. Be as specific as you can. Do your research at stores and trade shows and by asking friends. Then target your market, the people to whom you will be selling. All these demographic characteristics may not be relevant for your product, or you may need to include others.

37. What is the lifestyle and personality of your ideal customer? List findings and sources.

Buying habits _____

_____

_____

Lifestyle _____

_____

Personality _____

Leisure time _____

Other _____

_____

Today, people buy products not just because they need them, but because their purchases make them feel better about themselves or about a cause or an idea in which they believe.

38. What current and future market trends will influence your product? List findings and sources.

Economy _____

Location/traffic _____

_____

Seasonality _____

Sociocultural influences _____

_____

Trade laws _____

Other _____

You cannot design and manufacture in a "vacuum." It is essential to your business that you know and can tell potential buyers how your product fits into current and future market trends.

See "Market Research Form" on page 122.

- **Product Research**

39. Is your product unique?   **Yes / No**

40. Does it fill a void in the market?   **Yes / No**

41. Will it create a market for itself, by demand, because of its beauty, quality, uniqueness or practicality?   **Yes / No**

42. Is there a need for this design idea/fabrication?   **Yes / No**

© 1992, 1994 CHARLES BARSOTTI

"He's our Director of Design and Merchandising."

At least three, preferably four, of your answers should be yes. An 80 percent to 100 percent product viability factor is necessary if you are to compete successfully in the marketplace. Even though you may have a great idea and the first pieces are well received, does this mean that there is a true need for it in the marketplace and you should be giving serious thought to becoming a manufacturer?

By going to at least three retail venues, including online, that sell a product similar to yours, you can establish what the going market price is. You will need to make notes on variables such as quality of materials and construction and brand names versus off-brand names. Is your design/ product innovative compared to what is now on the market? Is it a unique product? If so, do your best to research the market price by looking for products that are closest to it in style, function and quality.

Identify each retail venue by name and indicate in which department of that store or website you found an item comparable to the one you are considering developing. It is important to know whether the sweater you are thinking of producing sells in the sportswear department or in better separates. Identifying the brand name of items similar to yours helps you to know who your competitors are. The fabrication (fabric) of which an item is made is another level of comparison. Let's say you are considering making toddler overalls in Polarfleece®. The only toddlers' overalls you find for sale are in corduroy. This fact can affect your research in several ways. For instance, is there no market for Polarfleece®? Are there no Polarfleece® overalls on the market because it is summertime? What is the difference in price between corduroy and Polarfleece® and how will this affect your costs?

If you plan to make higher quality overalls than what you have found in your survey, then your costs will be higher than the production costs for the items you have found. Are the features on the available overalls ones that you will include, or are the features you intend to use missing from the equivalent item? This also affects cost comparison.

Note the size range and color ways in which an item is offered. Do you plan to do the same or something different? Note the price (range) of comparable items. Make any comments about what you see.

Retail Venue #1

Venue name _____ Department _____

Brand name(s) of comparable product(s) _____

Fabrication _____

_____

Quality _____

Features _____

_____

Color ways _____

Size range _____ Price range _____

Comments _____

_____

Retail Venue #2

Venue name _____ Department _____

Brand name(s) of comparable product(s) _____

Fabrication _____

_____

Quality _____

Features _____

_____

Color ways _____

Size range _____ Price range _____

Comments _____

_____

Retail Venue #3

Venue name _____ Department _____

Brand name(s) of comparable product(s) _____

Fabrication _____

_____

Quality _____

Features _____

_____

Color ways _____

Size range _____ Price range _____

Comments _____

_____

43. What can you find out about your competition? List findings and sources.

What are the names of your competitors? _____

_____

What is their share of the market? _____

_____

What do you perceive as their strengths and weaknesses? _____

_____

Is the market overloaded or is there room for your product? _____

_____

Other _____

_____

You must know your competition by name, product category and, if possible, market share. You will use this information to tell potential buyers why they need to buy your product.

44. What are the benefits of your product?

Price _____

    Will it sell for about the same price as those now on the market?   **Yes / No**

    Will it sell at a higher than average market price?   **Yes / No**

Quality _____

Style _____

Fabrication _____

Other _____

    Is it an innovative product compared to what is now on the market?   **Yes / No**

Use your answers to place your product in the best market at the right price, because knowing about your product and its place in the market will give you the information you need to compete successfully. Your product may be able to sell at a price higher than current market value because of its design, materials or construction. But you cannot provide high quality and sell at a low price. Find your benefits, stay focused and develop products that achieve these benefits.

If you can identify four of your prospective customers' needs and how to meet them, you will be in the perfect position to be successful with your design-based product.

- **Positioning Statement**

After completing your analysis you will have a clear, focused vision of what your product is, who your ideal customers are and how your product will benefit them. Now you are ready to write your positioning statement. In seven to ten words, state why your product or service has value and why it should be purchased. This statement may develop into your slogan and will be used to introduce your company and product to potential buyers.

45. What is your positioning statement?

_____

_____

• **Sourcing and Costing**

Sourcing for materials and contractors or labor is the first step in calculating the cost of your product.

"I'll be glad when reptile skins are back in fashion!"

There are two main purposes for sourcing your materials and labor as part of your product development analysis and decision process. The most important is to establish the costs of producing one piece of your design or product. During this process you will automatically accomplish the second purpose by finding the sources you will need if you go ahead with your project and become a manufacturer.

Fabric and trims at wholesale prices can be obtained from mills, distributors and jobbers. Mills and distributors require large minimums; jobbers sell smaller quantities at slightly higher prices. Often, there is no continuity of fabric from a jobber.

Initially, you may be doing all the work in-house. When demand for your product increases, you may need to use outside contractors to meet production requirements. This can happen quickly and often sooner than you expect.

Once you have sources for materials and labor, you can calculate the cost of producing *one piece* of each design. In the garment industry, doubling this cost gives you a rough estimate of the wholesale price at which you will sell it. The final consumer will pay the retail price, which is double the wholesale price.

These topics are more thoroughly discussed in the following chapters:

Product Design (and Sourcing): Chapter 3

Calculating a Cost for Your Product: Chapter 4

Producing Your Product: Chapter 6

The End Result

If you have gotten to this point and are considering developing your product and possibly producing it, you

- have established your degree of participation in the development, production and selling of your product.
- have done some soul searching.
- have identified your market and your share of it.
- have researched the market value of comparable products.
- may have found an area(s) of weakness where you need help.

You have just finished a relatively brief run-through of the elements essential to deciding what it takes to be in the business of textile, apparel and sewn product manufacturing. You have completed the research necessary to go to the next step—dealing with the actual processes of product development, marketing and sales, and production. Possibly you have decided to try to sell your designs, not a product. By now, your ideas about your product and your involvement in its production should be clearer and more directed.

The rest of this book is a detailed discussion of the information and techniques necessary to stay in this business—successfully and profitably.

What you need to know to get started is right here, right now!

Read on, O Garmento!

CHAPTER 2: DEFINING THE IMAGE AND FORM OF YOUR COMPANY/PRODUCT

What's New

The information age and the Internet have created different silhouettes for business. The basic elements of design, marketing and sales, and production and distribution remain the same, although the profiles of these parts take some different shapes. Much of this is heady stuff for beginners in the business who design in the garage, source from jobbers, and produce and ship in small quantities. But it is most important to understand what new elements are driving the industry, because in just a few years they will become the norm through the trickle down effect. Some basic specifics to consider in your plan are described below.

E-commerce

E-commerce has several parts or players. The most obvious is the end consumer making an online purchase at sites like Amazon.com. You may research needlepoint restorers online and ultimately do business with a company you located through a search engine. Most companies have a Web presence as part of their marketing and advertising campaigns, even if they do not do business online. Additionally, e-commerce exists on a wholesale level involving purchases of supplies and materials online. Contract writing and negotiations are done by e-mail, usually with attached documents. A manufacturer may establish an extranet with its suppliers, labor sources, sales reps and distribution channels. This code-accessed association allows instant and free-flowing information to all parties, resulting in smoother operations for all involved. You must recognize and acknowledge the use of the Internet in all parts of your business to remain viable and competitive.

Horizontal Segments

A group comprised of only suppliers, or only contractors, or only designers, or only sales reps forms a horizontal segment within the business community. This segment may form an association or connect in some other way to further their interests, strengthen and enhance their businesses and promote themselves.

Vertical Structures

When all aspects of an entire industry or business—the manufacturer, its suppliers and contractors, marketing and sales components and distribution channels—form a unit, it is a vertical matrix. This structuring allows for the easy flow of information between parts to enhance on-time delivery of materials, production and shipments, as well as to allow salespeople access to the latest designs and up-to-the-minute delivery information.

Supply Chain Management

A major part of the effort to maintain total communication among all parts of a company is the development of SCM, in which information is gathered from and transferred to the appropriate parts of the organization or between organizations to create the timely and orderly supply of raw materials for the production and distribution of goods. Merchandisers work with (or are often also) designers, who drive the process by generating the need for specific goods to create and produce a line. Once the line is shipped, reorders must be filled. Anticipating and planning for all aspects of this process by utilizing the proper software helps to ensure a smooth(er) flow in the design-sales-production-distribution process.

Electronic Data Interface

In recent years EDI has come to dominate the fulfillment of orders. Bar codes are used on every item produced and packaged and/or on boxes of items. The information contained in these bar codes is electronically transmitted between the manufacturer and the seller (Liz Claiborne and Macy's) instead of an Advance Ship Notice or packing list. The store knows exactly what to expect in the delivery, and paperwork is reduced, as is the chance for error. Further advances in this technology now are in real time. Tracking is still done with bar codes, and if a problem arises this information is transmitted by a specific radio frequency, eliminating the data-input step and generating up-to-the-minute reports. For example, boxes of shirts should contain twelve per color in assorted sizes. The scanner catches a box with eleven shirts. This information is sent via a specific radio frequency within the plant, the box is pulled from the line and the problem is resolved before shipment. Headaches are reduced at every point of the distribution system.

Electronic Article Surveillance

EAS is a developing anti-theft technology that is expected to provide retailers with greater success in reducing losses from theft. The electronic codes have a small footprint and can be incorporated into woven and non-woven sewn-in tags and labels, paper hang tags and design elements of garments. Scanners at retail outlet exits read these codes and set off alarms as necessary.

The Business Plan

Most design-driven individuals have a very hard time putting their ideas into a business-plan format. It is often difficult to conceptualize and write the plan at the inception of your business. Many design-based manufacturers say, "I never had a plan; I just kept it all in my head." Or "I had a gut idea of what I wanted to do and how to succeed." This approach will work for a variable and limited amount of time. However, a realistic method of keeping you on track as you begin your design-based business is to have a written business plan to follow.

Made in America presents the basic elements of a business plan. As you work through this handbook you are actually working through, developing and defining your business plan. If some of the terms used in writing the plan do not make sense now, don't worry, they will. You will probably need to meet with an accountant or enrolled agent and a banker for their advice and input prior to submitting your business plan as part of the loan application. Also, there are many free publications on how to write a business plan available either from SCORE/the Small Business Administration or from the library.

The following are among the many reasons for writing a business plan:

- It forces you to delineate your business objectives and create a plan for reaching them in a specific amount of time.
- It's useful as a tool when discussing your business in a direct and organized manner with others.
- It helps in fulfilling marketing purposes.
- It's required as part of a loan application to a bank or commercial lender to obtain financing for your business.

Business Plan Outline

A. General Overview
    1. Legal structure (Explain your choice.)
        a. Sole Proprietorship
        b. Partnership
        c. Corporation

 2. Business type (Explain your choice.)
   a. Manufacturing
   b. Wholesale
   c. Retail
 3. What is the current market opportunity for your product?
 4. Why will you be successful?
B. Product Description
 1. What are the products being sold? (Describe them in detail.)
 2. What are the unique qualities of your product?
 3. At what wholesale or retail price(s) will your products sell?
C. Market Description
 1. What are the demographics of your ideal customers?
 2. What lifestyle and personality traits do they have?
 3. What factors will influence current and future market trends?
 4. Name and describe your competition. (Be specific.)
D. Marketing and Sales Plan
 1. Where and how will you sell your product? (Describe.)
 2. Who will sell your product?
 3. How will you market and advertise your product/service?
E. Design Development and Production Plan
 1. Who will design your products?
 2. Who will buy fabrics and trims?
 3. Who will produce your products/services?
 4. How will you pack and ship your orders?
 5. How will you handle marketing and sales?
 6. How will you handle collections?
F. Financial Data
 1. How much cash do you have/need to start your business? (Explain.)
 2. What are your sources of cash?
 3. What are the projected sales by month for three years? (Explain.)
 4. What is the projected cost of goods by month for three years? (Explain.)
 5. What are the expenses projected by month for three years? (Explain.)
 6. When do you project your business to show a profit? (Explain.)
G. Supporting Documents
 1. Personal resume
 2. Income statement for three years
 3. Line sheet
 4. Cost sheet
 5. Spec sheet

See "Business Plan" on page 139.

See "Income Statement" on page 119.

Protecting Your Business Name, Logo and Creativity

Be sure that your business name defines your product and your image. Other people in similar or different businesses may already be using the name you want to use. Business names are protected within each state by the filing of a fictitious-business-name or "doing business as" (dba) statement at county offices. Registered trade names, trademarks and servicemarks, filed with the federal government, protect your identity nationally and internationally. In both cases, searches can be done prior to application for the name or when the application for the name is submitted. The state searches can be done while you wait, sometimes online or by mail at most county fictitious-business-name offices. The national and international searches can be done at regional centers throughout the country that specialize in this information or you can hire a lawyer or other professional to find this information for you, prior to application. Increasingly, this information is online.

Fictitious Business Name/DBA

See the glossary definition. Generally, upon filing you pay a small fee, which protects your exclusive use of that name in your state. For instance, in California the business name is protected for five years and is renewable indefinitely. You must publish notice of your intent to use that name in a local paper, usually weekly for four weeks. In order to open a bank account in the name of your business you must submit proof of your fictitious business name. In some states these names are known as DBAs—Doing Business As.

URL

See the glossary definition. A URL or domain name is the online address for your web page. You must register your URL with InterNIC Domain Registration to gain ownership of the name. If no one has previously registered the name, it is yours with the payment of fees and the filing of forms. This is all done online and is often done by your webmaster, if you have one. There are a number of classifications available in addition to the ubiquitous ".com" for commercial ventures such as ".org" for organizations, ".edu" for educational institutions, ".net" for Internet network providers. Also, additional markings denote countries other than the United States. It is always best to have a URL that is the same as your business name—fictitious or otherwise, if possible. It is a good idea to have several choices of names to make sure you can have the same name for both your URL and your fictitious business name/DBA.

Trademark/Service mark

See the glossary definition. A trademark or service mark is the name or symbol used by a manufacturer or merchant to designate his goods and distinguish them from others. The trademark application is deceptively simple. Rules for the exact wording of what your business does and what the trademark represents and specific guidelines for the graphic presentation and representation of the logo must be adhered to. The holder of the trademark/service mark is obligated to protect the name and the quality of the product or service. The PTO (U.S. Patent and Trademark Office, 703-308-4357) and www.uspto.gov/ can be of help, as can *Trademark: How to Name Your Business and Product* from Nolo Press (800-992-6656 and www.nolo.com). And you can always hire a patent and trademark attorney to do this for you. It can take from one to three years to receive your trademark.

Copyright

See the glossary definition. A copyright is the exclusive right, granted by law, to make and dispose of copies of literary, musical or artistic work. Copyrights protect expression, and the copyright arises as soon as the original creation is fixed in expression—written, drawn, spoken. Whoever "fixes" the expression owns the copyright, whether it is created by that person or not. The more unusual and complex the expression, the more likely you are to receive a copyright. Textile designs and clothing are very difficult to copyright because the differences are subtle: changing the shape of a leaf or adding a pocket or changing a collar shape does not render the expression unusually or notably different. Also, basic common shapes, forms and other creative expressions are in the public domain. Registration of the copyright is mandatory prior to trying to enforce the copyright. You can register your designs or expressions as you produce them for $30 each; the copyright is issued in six to nine months or more. Copyrights can be registered retroactively if you have proof that you fixed your expression on a certain date.

Putting © and the date on a hangtag **qualifies for fixing the expression; it is not registration.** Registration requires filing the form and paying the fee. Once you have filed for a copyright, if you subsequently choose to enforce it, your costs will be limited to legal fees and court costs. If you file retroactively to the "fixing" of the expression, enforcement can cost thousands of dollars in legal and court fees. Copyright gives you the right to copy, distribute, create derivatives, publicly display and perform. It is necessary to decide if your expressions are sufficiently unusual or original to be copyrightable and if you wish to protect yourself against a possible infringement. In the garment business, as in all design-based operations, artistic license or taking your inspiration where you find it is the name of the game. Knockoffs, or copies of what you have created, are common. They can cause you distress or you can be flattered that someone found your designs worthy of reproduction. Money becomes the operative factor in deciding whether to pursue legal recourse. And that is something to consider only if your design is so unusual or complex that it is obvious that it has been copied. The citizen-friendly U.S. Copyright Office is reachable at 202-707-5000 and www.loc.gov/copyright/.

Patent

See the glossary definition. A patent is a government grant to an inventor for a stated period of time, conferring the exclusive right to make, use and sell an invention. A design patent is the only kind of patent you might ever use as a garment manufacturer. The process of obtaining one is long, and as with copyrights, you can do it yourself or obtain professional help. Call the Patent and Trademark Office (PTO) at 703-308-4357 and go to www.usppsto.gov.

"That may be your doodle Harry, but he's our intellectual property."

Sole Proprietorship, Partnership or Corporation

You will need to decide what legal form your business will take. The most common and simplest is the sole proprietorship. A **sole proprietorship** is a one-person unincorporated business. You have total control of and responsibility for the business (and its losses) and report your business income on your personal income tax returns. In the eyes of the law you and your sole proprietorship are one and the same.

If there is more than one major player in your business you will need to consider a **partnership**. A partnership is a business organization in which two or more people own the business. The typical business partnership is called a general partnership. Partners share control and management of the business, are liable for the obligations (including all debts) of the business and report their business income on their personal tax returns. There are also limited partnerships.

If you require legal and tax protections (and are prepared to pay annual fees) then forming a **corporation** is appropriate. A corporation is a legal entity that is separate and distinct from its owners. It can sue and be sued, it can incur debt and tax liabilities and it has a continuous life of its own—it will not dissolve when one of the partners leaves or when the owner decides to discontinue the business. A corporation is owned by shareholders who make decisions through a voting process. Your tax-filing status and procedures are determined by whether you are a C Corporation or an S Corporation.

These briefly described elements are parts of what can become a complex decision. You can obtain further information online, from the library, at a bookstore or from professionals. Nolo Press (800-992-6656 and www.nolo.com) has a series of excellent and informative do-it-yourself books on these subjects.

Professional Support

When you are first establishing your business, you should definitely consider talking with an attorney and an accountant or enrolled agent. She will point you in the most appropriate direction and make sure that you cover all bases and attend to all details in the beginning, not at crisis time after the fact. It might also be of value to consult with your insurance agent when you start your business; there may be some kinds of insurance you are required to have to operate your business legally. If and when your company's sales reach at least $2 million, it is time to consider using a factor. See the glossary definition. The use of a factor at the right time can make your cash flow much easier. Money will be fronted or lent to you for operating expenses based on your receivables—orders waiting to be filled, shipped and billed. Creditors will always be paid on time. The factors will, of course, charge a fee for their services, but you still get your profits, with fewer headaches because of a smoother operation.

Safely Selling Your Design Ideas

What You Need

Whether you are a designer of clothing, accessories, textiles, sewn products or other fashion/ sewn items, you might prefer to simply create and **sell the designs** and not manufacture them. Selling your designs can be an income-producing venture. You will need the following:

- Well-established contacts in the field, from previous work or social relationships, for marketing your designs.
- A constant flow of good current designs.
- An impressive portfolio of your design work.
- Preferably, solid work experience as a designer in your chosen field/medium.

The Deal

As a freelance designer you may sell your designs outright for a flat fee, relinquishing owner- ship and further claims, or you may license them. Under a licensing arrangement you retain own- ership and collect future royalties that are deducted from money paid to you at the beginning of the contract. The percentage of royalties is determined by gross sales within a time frame. There are some standard legal forms for this. You can also consult an attorney who will write a contract for you; this contract will protect your interests and detail negotiable and non-negotiable items specific to each sale. In future deals you can fill in the spaces appropriate to the circumstances. Having a contract that can be used repeatedly with minor changes can be a very cost-effective way to clearly protect yourself and your future as a freelance designer. Tell your attorney this is the type of contract you wish to have.

Confidential Disclosure Agreements

Whenever you show your designs to anyone it is very important to protect yourself. When someone is interested enough in your creative expression to make an offer or talk money, it is easy to get caught up in the excitement of the moment and not think clearly. Confidential disclo- sure agreements will help ensure that the people and companies to whom you show your designs and products will not look at your work, say they are not interested and then turn around and knock off or copy your designs. If someone is unwilling to sign such an agreement, do not show them your work or do business with them.

See "Confidential Disclosure Agreement" on page 121.

Business Licenses, Permits and Sales Tax

It is important to check with your local government—city or county—as to **zoning** require-ments and restrictions for operating a business, particularly within the home. Additionally, many states require registration of garment manufacturers and have laws that restrict where garments can be manufactured. (*See "Garment Manufacturer's License and Registration" on page 49.*) Only if your place of business is located in an unincorporated area of the county do you get **permits and licenses** from the county; otherwise, you get them from the city or town where your business is actually located. If you have a fictitious business name registered with the state, many commu-nity or county licensing offices will want to see proof of that. Also bring documentation of your social security number and/or federal tax ID number; some offices may want to see your driver's license. If it is illegal to manufacture garments or accessories in a residence in your state, your office and design studio can be in the home but actual manufacturing must be done elsewhere. You should identify your business as a service, as a designer or as the business office of a manu-facturing company: again, your office is in the home but manufacturing is done elsewhere. Also, there may be **zoning** issues to consider. Call the **business license** office in your community or county, as appropriate, for information.

In any state that has a sales tax you will need a **resale license** so that you can purchase your raw materials without paying tax on them. You must give this license number to any supplier within the state where you do business and from whom you are purchasing materials for resale—a wholesaler, jobber or retailer. You will also need to get these numbers from any store or catalog that is within the state where you do business and to whom you are selling goods without collect-ing sales tax. A resale license is not a license to *just purchase* materials at wholesale prices. You must be able to show proof that these goods, purchased with a resale number, are used in manu-facturing or creating items for resale. The sales tax is collected at the point of final sale, the end consumer.

If you do make direct sales to consumers, it is required by law that you collect the sales tax on the purchase price as part of the money you collect from the consumer. When you report your resale activity (monthly, quarterly or annually, depending upon your total gross sales) you indicate what, if anything, you have sold on which you have collected tax. You then send the collected tax to the state when you file your periodic return to the resale tax office.

The issues concerning the collection of interstate sales tax have yet to be resolved. In fact, they are becoming even more complex with the explosive growth of e-commerce. If you sell by catalog or e-commerce to end consumers in other states, you may ultimately (and fairly soon) be responsible for charging, collecting and depositing the sales taxes you have collected. This may apply to many of the states to which you ship orders within the U.S.

Business Identity

The ideas you formulate in this process of identifying you and your business are the basis from which you will continually develop the thoughts and action that become your business identity. Your product is the driving force behind your identity. Business cards, letterhead, tags, ads, flyers, line sheets (and all other printed materials) and websites will be following your image. Be creative. Have fun. The following are your guidelines:

Logo

Your logo can be a graphic only or a name only or both a graphic and a name. It should be as representative of the image you wish to project and your product as possible. It should be eye-catching and memorable.

You can develop your own logo using available computer clip art and font software. You can develop one with the help of a graphic artist. Or you can combine both methods. However you do it, the logo should be concise and graphically reproducible in a clear way—by both commercial and computer printers or other forms of visual reproduction such as online graphics. The more information, visual and otherwise, you can supply to the graphic artist, the quicker and better the resulting output from her. Collect pictures, symbols—anything that has a look or feel you like—and bring them to your graphic artist. Get copies of typefaces or fonts that you like. If you have a very definite sense of what you want, sketch it as best you can. All of this will give your graphic artist a place from which to start.

Before you head to the graphic artist, spend time visualizing or imagining the kind of impact your graphic images will have and responses you might expect as a result of that impact. You want people to remember your company and what you do and you want them to identify your company and your product with that image—always. When thinking about what form your logo might take, bear that in mind.

Because your logo will appear on your business cards, letterhead and envelopes, brochures, possibly order forms, invoices and statements, hangtags, labels, website and in advertising, simplicity and clarity are very important. Of course, the aesthetics of the image/word combination must be very pleasing to you, since it is the image you will use to represent your company and products. As always, when choosing a professional, make sure she is someone with whom you have easy communication. Ask to see samples of the graphic artist's work to get a good sense of her style and abilities. Before you begin work, establish whether you will pay by the hour or by the job and who decides when the job is finished.

Choosing Your Logo....

Old Santa   Young Santa

Color

The use of color in your logo, stationery, brochures, ordering and billing forms, labels and tags is another way to make a statement and/or evoke a response from prospective buyers of your product.

Colored ink can be used with white stock or in combination with colored paper stock. Colored ink costs will be more than black ink. If you have some flexibility in your color range and time frame, your printer should be able to run your work when he is already printing—for someone else—a color that is acceptable to you. Obviously, you cannot be too exacting in your color choice if you try to use this method of cutting costs, which avoids the setup charge for a specific color. Also, when it comes time to reprint, you will have to choose whether to pay the setup charge for a specific color or to print your current materials in a look different than your first run.

Paper stock in all weights and formats is available in a wide variety of colors and textures. Both cost and aesthetics are major factors, in addition to quality. If you want business cards, letterhead, envelopes, brochures and tags all on paper with the same color and finish, make sure you indicate that to the printer at the beginning of your paper "interview." Not all paperweights or finishes or forms are available in any given color. And these days, papers come and go rapidly; they are very fashionable! Color printing and images can also be reproduced with color copy machines. As a rule, this is quite costly and should be used in a limited way.

You can do color printing on a computer. Some people print out their letterhead and envelopes as they need them. It is definitely a cost-effective, though not time-effective, way of creating colored printed paper. Whether this is a practical method for you depends on how much stationery you will actually be using. For example, will you be doing large mailings using many envelopes or pieces of stationery? If so, then you will want to use preprinted stock.

As you are undoubtedly aware, many books have been written on the subject of what various colors symbolize or the feelings, moods or emotions they evoke. You have experienced that the color blue is calming and red is exciting. Use the effect colors have on people in a purposeful way when you design your look, logo or letterhead. And remember to *follow the image of your company.*

Website

A website is an announcement to the Internet-savvy public of your products and your company. It can also serve as a detailed catalog of the items in your line(s). And of course it can be a sales venue for your product lines.

It is a relatively simple process to obtain a URL, sign up with an Internet Service Provider (ISP), build a web page, be listed with appropriate search engines and be hot-linked to other sites. If you cannot do this yourself, there are many people who can set this up for you. Also, the major ISPs (AOL and Earthlink, for example) offer software to build a simple web page. The important thing is to go for the exposure as soon as possible, even if your product line is not firm or you are still sourcing for a particular fabric or contractor. Get your name and logo out there! Follow the image of your company and use your positioning statement if you wish.

Business Card

Your business card is the item most often used to identify you and your business. You want people to save yours and *call you* to do business. It should be as clear, informative and eye-catching as possible. You definitely must include the following information on your business card:

• Logo	• Street address	• Cell phone number with area code
• Company name	• City, state, zip code	• Pager number with area code
• Your name	• Phone number with area code	• Web site/URL
• Description of business	• Fax number with area code	• E-mail address

Labels, Hangtags, Size and Care Tags

These items, which are sewn or attached to your product with plastic tag-attachers or other methods, provide information about your company and your product: all the information you want to give your customers and all the information various laws **require** you to give your customers (fiber content, country of origin of fabric and manufacture of product, company name or RN number and care instructions).

Labels are usually fabric and sewn into the neck or waist seam of apparel, or at appropriate locations on other items. The labels are either woven or printed. Generally, your logo and company name appear on the label.

Hangtags are printed on card stock. In addition to your company name and logo, your business address in full or just the city and state, as well as a website address, can be printed on the tag. A hangtag can also provide style, size, color and fabric information. If sewn labels and tags are not appropriate to your product, hangtags are the way to get all the necessary information on each item. Separate size tags and care tags can be sewn tags or hangtags.

Letterhead and Envelopes

Your letterhead and envelope are also important presentations of your image and your company. They should include all the information on your business card.   A printer, your computer or just a rubber stamp can print your letterhead. As mentioned above, quality, quantity and end use are the determining factors.

CHAPTER 3: PRODUCT DESIGN

Having a great design idea has brought you this far. Take a minute to study the Design Idea Flow Chart that follows and familiarize yourself with how the design process develops from your initial ideas to a successful sale of the actual product. As you take the steps to turn your design idea into a reality, remember to remain responsive to all the feedback you will receive while maintaining your own sense of aesthetics and design.

Market Research

As we discussed in Section 1: Evaluating Your Skills and Product for Development, doing your market research provides you with information essential to the development of your product for your target market. Whether you already have a strong idea of your product and market or are still defining either or both areas, be sure that you have the appropriate product for the appropriate market.

See "Market Research Form" on page 122.

"Does your new market research team walk, or just crawl?"

Design Idea Flow Chart

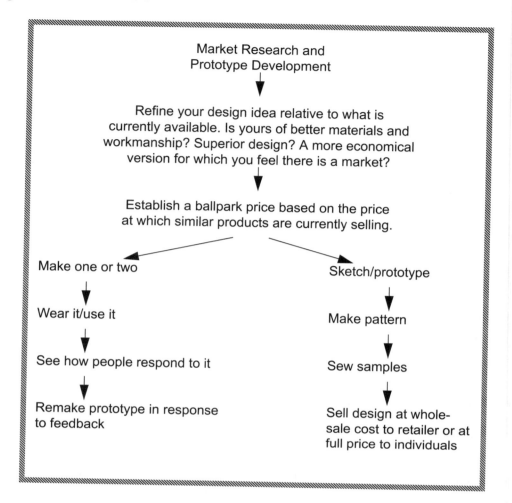

Market Research and
Prototype Development

↓

Refine your design idea relative to what is
currently available. Is yours of better materials and
workmanship? Superior design? A more economical
version for which you feel there is a market?

↓

Establish a ballpark price based on the price
at which similar products are currently selling.

Make one or two

↓

Wear it/use it

↓

See how people respond to it

↓

Remake prototype in response
to feedback

Sketch/prototype

↓

Make pattern

↓

Sew samples

↓

Sell design at whole-
sale cost to retailer or at
full price to individuals

Product Line

Product line is the operative word (or phrase, in this case) in thinking about product design. A product line consists of individual designs or products that work together to create a look or image that will sell for a prescribed amount of time. This cohesive collection of design ideas—for a season, for example—is what you use as the focal point for the development of your designs and subsequently for selling purposes. You create a look: a collection that is held together by silhouette, color, fabrication or theme—or any or all of these.

- Most likely, if you are using this handbook, *your design ideas* are what are driving you to produce or manufacture a product.

- Follow your sense of design.

- Be aware of fashion trends—either to follow, purposely ignore, avoid or break away from.

- Know your target market—your high-end evening wear will not sell to the K Mart crowd.

- Maximize the various attributes of the fabrics you use—pattern, texture, color range, draping qualities, washability.

- Be aware of the differences between designing for production and designing one of a kind.

- Specific inspiration is generally from silhouette to fabric or fabric to silhouette. In the garment business, finding the right or suitable fabrics will be the biggest challenge for first-time designers. Often you cannot find or cannot afford what you want, so you design "into" the available piece goods. Taking your lead from the fabric, you adapt your design to maximize its look when made up in that available fabric.

- Have an adequate number of product choices so that the line looks full and complete. Create enough similar items that have a cohesive theme so that the store or catalog buyer has a sufficient array from which to select items appropriate to her clientele.

"Word from above is:
sun yellow is the color of the season."

Color Forecasting

It can be frustrating to have your color sense overridden by a forecast made by committee a year and a half to three years previously. But this is how the mills determine what color yarns to make and fabrics to weave well in advance of the demands of manufacturers a year or two down the line. The forecasters of both colors and textiles pay heed to aesthetic issues, color theories, economic, political and social factors and trends, and some standards for specific markets and seasons. Holiday time is glittery, with gold, silver, red, green and blue predominating. Pastels for infants and bold colors for kids are always a safe bet, although there are fashion-forward variations. But then there are winter white and summer white. Oh my, what to do! Pay attention to the forecasts *and* your own design sense. Some prominent forecasters are Pantone Color Institute

(201-935-5500), Cotton Incorporated (212-413-8300), Promostyl (212-921-7930), The Color Association of the United States (212-582-6884) and Pat Tunsky Inc. (212-944-9160).

 Tips for Developing Your Product Line

- Have from three to five styles/silhouettes per season.
- Each style should be offered in two to four fabrications—colors, prints, fabrics.
- Have a full size range appropriate to the item:
    - Women's dresses should be sizes 2-14.
    - An oversize sweatshirt can be one-size-fits-all.
    - Men's boxer shorts can be S, M, L, XL.
    - Infants' clothing should be 0 - 3 months, 3 - 6 months, 6 - 12 months, etc.
- Initially, focus on one part of the market share, one type of buyer who buys this type of merchandise: just infants, not infants *and* toddlers; just accessories, not clothing *and* accessories.
- Offer a balance of style types in a line, such as a typical 2-to-1 ratio of tops to bottoms.
- Have a spec sheet for each design.

Initial Design Specification Sheets

These sheets contain all the information about each style you are designing and expect to produce for each season. They become the "bible" for the production of each style. Use one sheet for each style you are considering for your current line. Keep the sheets together in a notebook (with your Fabric/Trim Spec Sheets and Cost Sheets). The following information must be included on each sheet.

- style name
- style number
- colors/fabrications
- size range

- fabric and trim swatches
- prices of materials
- line drawing
- number of pattern pieces

See "Initial Design Spec Sheet" on page 124.

See "Initial Design Spec Sheet" on page 124.

The Prototype

The prototype is the first creation of the item you are designing. It may come even before an actual pattern is made. It can be a mock-up of what you want the item to look like or it can be the first sample sewn together. If you have a prototype, you or the patternmaker will use that as the basis for pattern making. If you do not have a prototype, you will need sketches from which to make a pattern. Refining the prototypes of each design, especially when you are developing your product line, is a process that must be done thoroughly step-by-step.

"Sorry, I'm the angel of garment design. The angel
of accessory design is over there."

You personally may be able to take a design from your idea to a prototype, but you cannot expect a patternmaker to do the same. Patternmakers are visual people and need to see some sort of image for which they are creating a pattern. Even if you do not draw as well as you would like to, sketch your idea. Don't worry if it isn't a museum-quality work of art! You just want to give the patternmaker an idea of what you have in mind. You might also use a fashion illustrator or artist who may be able to work from your verbal description and can certainly work from your sketch. This illustration or drawing should be in sufficient detail for the patternmaker to create all the elements that you have in mind: darts, pockets, collar, length, fitted waist.

The prototype may go through several stages of until it looks right, makes up right and actually becomes the first sample. It should be tried on a real body to test for fit and functionality. You want it to look as good as possible and function as well as possible before you make the final pattern. After any iterations of the initial prototype have been refined sufficiently, the finished pattern and finished sample are completed. So, often a prototype and a selling or production sample are one and the same. The cost of prototype development can be high; it can run $1,000 in San Francisco, for example. This figure may also include the cost of grading a pattern, which is usually not done until sales figures determine whether or not a style will be put into production and consequently into a full size range. (*See "Making Markers" on page 80.*)

CAD and CAM

Computer-aided design (CAD) has eliminated many of the time-consuming and repetitive elements of design and patternmaking and streamlined both. Of course, the software is only as good as its user, so it is still essential to work with a skilled and experienced patternmaker. Computer-aided manufacturing (CAM) handles the entire production operation. Again, the human links in the process are the key to the success of the operation.

Patterns and Patternmakers

As you develop your patterns, it is important to focus on patterns that "are" your look. You can use these same patterns repeatedly, season after season—changing the fabric or collar shape, adding a pocket or a bow, removing a pleat or adding a slit to a skirt. These simple changes give you a new look each season and save you the time and money of creating new patterns every season. Your line needs an enduring identity *and* your line needs something fresh for each new selling season. You can try out one or two completely new designs each season without much hassle, but the majority of your line should be simple—an easy updating of existing patterns.

Unless you become a major couture house, where dramatic change from season to season rules, your selling point and your profitability remain in reusing your successful patterns. You must identify and usually eliminate those designs whose ratio of cost to selling price is not a profitable one. Sometimes you may want to keep an item in your line that does not meet the profitability ratio because it fills out or completes your line even though it sells to a narrow market. The loss on an unprofitable item can be offset by the extreme profitability of a best-selling item.

Production patterns differ from home-sewing patterns in several important characteristics:

- They use as few pattern pieces as possible and keep construction simple without losing the integrity of the design. Cutting fewer pieces and sewing together fewer pieces lowers cutting and labor costs.

- Production patterns do include seam allowances but there is no seam allowance line actually indicated on the pattern or marked on the cut pieces of fabric. The actual measurement for the seam allowance (3/8", for example) is written on the pattern itself and on the written instructions given to the sewers. The 5/8" seam allowance used in home-sewing patterns is not an industry standard.

- Notches, used to identify where pieces are joined or lined up, are cut into (not protruding from) the pattern piece with a special notcher. Notches on the cut pieces are marked with a slit (or two or three) about ¼" deep into the seam allowance.

- All pattern pieces are cut on the flat; none are ever cut on a fold in production cutting. Therefore, all pattern pieces must be the full piece, never half the piece to be cut on a fold.

Patternmakers must know how to make patterns for "first (prototype) through production." They must be able to develop the prototype and fine-tune it into a workable pattern for samples and then for a production pattern. The sample pattern and the production pattern may be the same. The production pattern will have to be graded—made in the full size range—once you have orders. Grading patterns is a sophisticated process, done by hand or CAD, to increase/decrease seams, darts, pleats, and so on, in the correct ratios to achieve proper fit in each size. Also, sometimes a style may lose its good looks when made into a larger or smaller size. Experienced designers, sample makers and graders generally know how to prevent this problem from occurring. Creating patterns that are workable for production sewing, accurate for fit and true to your ideas can be accomplished in a number of ways.

- If you have the expertise to create patterns that meet these requirements, then the next step is yours. Remember to identify each pattern piece by style number and size and indicate the number of pieces to cut per garment (four pocket pieces, for example).

- It is possible to adapt packaged patterns, available at fabric stores, to your own designs. To do this you must have some understanding of pattern making. For example, if you are planning to eliminate darts, will you maintain the form-fitting nature of the pattern in another way, such as open pleats? Will you manipulate other pattern elements to change its form-fitting nature? Additionally, you need to know which elements of garment construction are the most time- and cost-effective in production sewing; it is essential to create an item that goes together easily, economically and uses the fewest number of pieces possible. As a patternmaker, you must make those decisions yourself; you cannot ask a sewing contractor or production sewer to solve these problems for you, although their input is invaluable. So, if you are not an accomplished patternmaker who is able to work with all these parameters, you will need to use a professional patternmaker. Remember, production sewing and home sewing are like tigers and house cats. Same family, exaggerated characteristics.

- To find a professional patternmaker, ask other designers and manufacturers or a contract sewing shop for recommendations. Look in the Yellow Pages under Patternmakers—Clothing. If you use people who have not been personally recommended, ask to see samples of their work and get the names of clients for whom they have done pattern making. Check references.

Usually, patternmakers also grade patterns in an entire size range, size 2-14, for example. Do not grade a pattern until you are ready to go into production with it, because grading is costly. Have the sample pattern(s) made in the size you wish to use for sales and display purposes— probably a small size to save on fabric costs. Sometimes a particular style looks best in a smaller or larger size. Let aesthetics be your guide. You want these samples to look their best!

Tips on Making Your Own Patterns

- Make your first patterns in brown kraft or similar-weight paper.
- Date each pattern and each revision.
- For each style, include a spec sheet. *See "Initial Design Spec Sheet" on page 124.*
- Once you have taken all the kinks out of the patterns and you know they work in production, then you can make them out of poster board or tag board.
- Hang your patterns from a rack, keeping all pieces of each pattern together and separate from other styles. If you do your own cutting, you may also want to separate all the pattern pieces of each size of each style. Use a ¾" hole punch and pattern-hanging hooks to hang and store patterns.
- Keep all your patterns; you might turn a failure into a best-selling design.

A (Very) Short Primer in Textiles

Terminology

BOTTOM WEIGHT—A weight of fabric suitable for pants, skirts, jackets and similar items.

CARE INSTRUCTIONS—Specifics of water temperature, type of soap, hand or machine washing and drying method, or instructions to dry clean only. Manufacturers are required to list instructions for one preferred method of care.

EMBOSSED—A finish created by a raised design on the surface of the fabric.

FABRIC—Any cloth made by weaving, knitting or felting from fibers or thread.

FABRIC COUNT—Used for woven goods: warp ends per inch times weft ends per inch.

FABRIC FINISHES—A variety of mechanical and chemical methods used to achieve a certain look, feel or quality. For example, stonewashing for a well-worn look, waterproofing, or other techniques to create a "denim" look for fabric that is not a true denim due to weave and fiber differences.

FIBER—The fundamental component of any substance that can be separated into threads and used to assemble a textile yarn or fabric.

FIBER CONTENT—The percentage of each fiber in a fabric. For example, 100 percent cotton or 50 percent cotton/50 percent polyester.

GENERIC NAME—The common or family name for a natural or manufactured fiber must appear on the fiber content label. For example, spandex is the generic name; LYCRA® is a trademarked spandex by Dupont.

GLAZED—A finish that coats the fabric with a substance to create a glossy surface.

HAND—The feel of a fabric.

KNIT—A cloth made of interlocking loops of yarn. Single knits include jersey and rib; double knits include interlock.

LAB DIP—A test sample of a specific dye on a specific fabric.

MICROFIBER—(1) Very-fine-filament or long-fine yarn, generally nylon, polyester or a blend. (2) Fabric made of these fibers.

NAP/PILE—The downy or hairy surface of cloth formed by short fibers or by brushing the fabric surface.

PIECE GOODS (YARD GOODS)—Textiles made in standard widths.

TOP WEIGHT—A weight of fabric suitable for blouses, shirts and similar items.

WARP—The lengthwise yarns or fibers in a weaving process.

WEFT/FILL—The crosswise yarns or fibers in a weaving process.

WOVEN—Fabric produced by weaving or interlacing threads/yarns at right angles. The three basic weave structures are plain, twill and satin.

For a complete listing of textile terminology refer to a fabric dictionary. (*See "Appendix A: Bibliography" on page 109.*)

Burning Characteristics of Major Fiber Types

FIBER TYPE	NEAR FLAME	IN FLAME	REMOVED FROM FLAME	ODOR OF SMOKE	TYPE OF RESIDUE
Asbestos, glass	No effect	Glows	No change	None	NA
Cellulosic, such as cotton, line viscose, lyocell	Curls	Burns fiercely	Burns, can glow, smolders	Like burning wood, leaves, paper	Soft, gray ash
Silk	No effect	Burns slowly	Tends to go out	Like burning feathers	Crushable ash
Wool	No effect	Burns slowly	Tends to go out	Like burning hair or meat	Crushable ash
Acetate, triacetate	Curls	Burns, melts	Burns, melts	Like vinegar	Crushable bead
Acrylic	Shrinks away	Burns, melts	Burns, melts	Fishy	Breakable bead
Modacrylic	Shrinks away	Burns, melts	Goes out	Like animal waste!!	Breakable bead
Nylon	Shrinks away	Melts, drips	Tends to go out	Possibly like celery seed	Hard bead
Olefin (polypropylene)	Shrinks away	Burns, melts, black smoke	Burns, melts	Like wax	Hard bead
Polyester	Shrinks away	Burns, melts	Tends to go out	Possibly aromatic	Hard bead

The State of the Craft

The production of fabrics is a complex, constantly evolving process. Fabrics are woven (yarns/ threads intersect at right angles), knitted (loops of yarn interlock) or nonwoven (a fiber web of some type is formed by a chemical or mechanical process). New fibers, new technologies for dyeing and color matching and the demands of the fashion market ensure a constant evolution of looks, finish and color palettes. For instance, one dye used on a woven fabric made from a combination of fibers—such as cotton warp and acetate weft—can produce a multicolored result because the cotton warp will dye green and the acetate weft yellow. Blends of fibers such as 50 percent cotton/ 50 percent polyester produce fabrics that for the most part retain the hand and look of cotton and the easy-care qualities of polyester. Lab dips and the hand of the fabric remain the final say on what works and what does not. Of course, durability is desirable!

Highly technical fabrics—created with modern technology and space-age fibers—are used in art and for the body by couturiers and fashion-forward designers. These fabrics are not necessarily comfortable to wear but they each have qualities—stiffness, pleats, fluidity, for instance—that allow designers like Issey Miyake to manifest designs of unique construction, execution and artistry.

As with all aspects of the U.S. garment industry, much fabric sourcing has shifted to offshore suppliers, many of whom exhibit at fabric trade shows in this country.

Informative classes on textiles are offered at community colleges, fabric stores and trade show seminars.

For detailed information on textiles: *See "Appendix A: Bibliography" on page 109.*

The Fabric and Trim Search

Usually, you will have a design idea and then search for the fabrics you have envisioned as the best ones to create the look you want. If your dream fabrics are not available, you must use what is available for your existing designs or change the designs to better accommodate the fabrics you can use. Fortunately, fabric often serves as the inspiration for your designs so this is not a bad situation in which to find yourself. Flexibility is the optimum mode. The key words in this section are **"in the quantities you need," "throughout the manufacturing season"** and **"at wholesale prices."** There is no way to make a profit if you purchase fabric at retail prices from a fabric store. Occasionally, you may do so for expediency—to make samples or for a special order or because you need just a small quantity to finish an order. If your supplier is out of stock or you cannot wait until the fabric arrives, utilizing the fabric store as an immediate resource is a good idea. These things do happen. But for economic sense and sanity it is best to keep these purchases to an absolute minimum. Be sure to request a discount from fabric retailers based upon your sales and reuse tax number. (This ensures that you will not pay tax on your purchase and it may entitle you to a discount.) Assume that wholesale fabric costs will be about 50 percent of **full** nondiscounted retail prices.

For sample making, purchase enough fabric, including interfacing, lining and trim to make sufficient samples for sales purposes. These will include what you need to take to trade shows, on selling trips or for sales reps. You should also have an extra set or two for other sales and publicity purposes.

When you manufacture product to fill your first orders, more than likely the production run will be small and consequently, you will again be looking for small quantities of materials. If you make accessories or infant clothing, you will obviously be purchasing smaller quantities of fabric to produce your orders than a women's sportswear line would require, for instance.

So, for a while, you need to find fabrics and trim

- that you can purchase in small quantities at wholesale prices
- that have continuity of availability for the season
- which, if demand necessitates, you can obtain in larger quantities throughout the season.

Tips on Fabric and Trim Sourcing

- Burn tests are a simple way of checking questionable fiber content. (*See "Burning Characteristics of Major Fiber Types" on page 40.*)
- When doing business with a fabric supplier by phone, fax or e-mail, always request that swatches be sent to you. *Never purchase yardage or trim without <u>seeing and feeling</u> a sample of exactly what you are buying.* Everyone perceives color differently—what you call navy blue someone else may call royal blue. Also, you need to check the hand, weight and quality of the fabric. Many companies will overnight the swatches to you, particularly if you are a regular customer.
- As you begin your sourcing, do so with an eye to developing a business relationship with several suppliers of the fabrics and trims you use so that you have choices based on availability, price, color and so on. You may prefer a particular fabric, but it may not always be available when you need it. Protect yourself by building a strong "army" of suppliers and contractors.
- If you will be using bias tape or cording, order sufficient fabric to have your own bias tape or cording made to your specifications so they will match your fabric. A less expensive and better finished product will result if you have the items made from your own fabric rather than purchasing ready-made trims. To calculate how much fabric to order for this purpose, you will need to contact whoever will be making the cord or trim to find out how many yards of trim you will get from fabric of a specific width.
- WATCH DYE LOTS! All fabric of each color must be exactly the same color. You cannot produce a dress with sleeves in two different shades of wine red. Make sure all fabric of each color you order is from the same dye lot. Of course, when you reorder fabric, you will almost surely get a different dye lot.
- How much extra fabric should you order? Some fabrics are highly flawed, such as cotton interlock, and some are always just about perfect. Once you have worked with specific fabrics from specific manufacturers, you will know what percentage of overage you need to deal with fabric

flaws. Also, you may always want to order 5-10 percent more extra fabric than you need, to deal with undershippage or other unknowns.

• If you think or know that you will be getting reorders of a particular style in a particular fabric, order sufficient fabric initially so that you have no concerns about dye lots, availability, and continuity. Either way you are taking a chance: that you'll have unused fabric in inventory or that the fabric you need will be available when you need it. You can always promote an item as available in "limited quantities": no unused fabric inventory, no concerns about getting more fabric. Of course, if it is a bestseller, you will probably try and scramble up suitable fabric to make more goods.

"Come back here with that basket of all my fabrics!"

© 1993,1994 LEO CULLUM

Fabric Trade Shows

There are a number of places and ways to find the fabrics you want at wholesale prices, in the small quantities you need for samples and when your company and your output are small. There are two kinds of fabric trade shows: One is geared to larger manufacturers and the other to smaller manufacturers and fabric stores. Often mills or distributors of fabrics have two sales divisions, each geared to a different market but both selling substantially the same goods with a slight difference in price and a major difference in the minimum order.

Shows such as the International Fashion Fabric Exposition in New York and the Los Angeles International Textile Show aim at the larger manufacturers. Minimum orders can be a thousand yards per color of fabric, or more. Most of the major mills represented at these shows will not be available to address your needs. Some jobbers or smaller mills may welcome you with open arms.

There will be an incredibly large selection of fabrics available, if you meet the minimums and credit measures.

Sewing and craft shows are held in different cities each fall and spring. (The International Textiles and Sewing Expo is held twice a year in Las Vegas.) These shows cater to buyers of smaller wholesale quantities. Prices might be slightly higher than those at the manufacturers' shows, but you can buy in the quantities you actually need. You may well be a big customer to some of the companies selling at these shows. There will be many jobbers selling small quantities and odd lots of fabric.

Occasionally, the larger mills might sell to you on a continuing basis out of their sample rooms—the part of the company that deals with supplying sample yardage which manufacturers and designers use to make up their sample goods for sales purposes. You need to know your seasonal needs fairly accurately for this to work. (*See "Fabric Shows and Garment Manufacturing Shows" on page 115.*)

Often the layout of a fabric trade show seems to make little sense, although the trims are usually in a distinct section, separate from the fabrics. The trade show directory generally organizes the listings in several ways: alphabetically by company name, numerically by booth number, and by categories of goods sold (cottons, bottomweights, prints, etc.). So if you are looking for cotton twill, you would go to booths listed under cotton and bottomweights, for example.

Year-Round Fabric Sources

Jobbers are available to you year-round, not just at trade shows. They will sell you small quantities at good prices. Lack of continuity of supply is the drawback of dealing with a jobber. Probably a jobber will only have stock on hand in any fabric, so if you want availability of fabric for a full season, using a jobber will not work. An alternative is to offer limited production runs of a particular design in a particular fabric. Some jobbers do have continuity in some "basic" fabrics and colors. Local jobbers can be found in the Yellow Pages under <u>Fabric—Wholesale & Manufacturers.</u>

There are national and regional source books of fabric and trim. (*See "Year-Round Fabric and Industry Information" on page 113.*) You can use these books and your telephone to find the fabrics you need and request swatches when appropriate. If the fabric shows are months and miles away and you really need to see what is available, visit your local fabric stores; look around and write down mill names from selvage edges or bolt ends. It is a place to start. Remember: (1) Except in an emergency, you cannot afford to buy yardage from a fabric store because you will be paying retail prices for fabric and trim when you should be paying wholesale. (2) There is no way you can be profitable and stay in business if you purchase your materials at retail, and (3) Never buy fabric without seeing and handling a swatch.

Fabric/Trim Specification Sheets

This sheet contains all the information you must have about any fabric you are using or considering using. Use a separate sheet for each fabric you are considering for your current line. Keep them together in a notebook (with your Initial Design Spec Sheets and Cost Sheets). The following information must be included on each sheet.

- vendor, contact name
- address and phone number
- prices
- window of availability
- lead times

- swatches
- fiber content
- available colors
- fabric width
- fabric care instructions

See "Fabric/Trim Spec Sheet" on page 125.

Labels

Labels provide many kinds of necessary information for consumers: name of manufacturer, country of origin, size, fabrication and care instructions.

Fiber Content and Country of Origin

The complete fiber content (the percentage of each fiber in the fabric), country of origin of the fabric, and the country of manufacture of the garment must also appear on a permanent, legible, accurate tag or label. Detailed information, "Threading Your Way Through the Labeling Requirements Under the Textile and Wool Acts," is available at www.ftc.gov/bcp/conline/pubs/buspubs/thread.htm.

Care

According to Federal Trade Commission rules, manufacturers and importers of textile wearing apparel and specified piece goods are required to provide a permanent, legible, accurate tag or label presenting regular care instructions and information. Since the inception of these rules in 1972, a series of symbols have developed to cover washing, bleaching, drying, ironing and dry-cleaning. A detailed pamphlet, "Writing a Care Label," is available online at www.textilecare.com/writing/htm. "Clothing Care Symbol Guide" is available online at www.ftc.gov/bcp/conline/pubs/products/cln-card.pdf.

Manufacturing Services

Within the production pipeline there are a variety of services that cover all phases of the design and manufacturing process. The auxiliary services help with designing, sample making, pattern making, shipping and distribution.

Auxiliary Services

- **DESIGNERS**—People who create textile, apparel and sewn product designs.
- **PATTERNMAKERS**—People who make patterns for use in the manufacture of apparel and sewn products.
- **SAMPLE MAKERS**—People who sew the prototypes, first samples, selling and production samples.
- **PATTERN GRADERS**—Individuals or contractors who create pattern pieces in a full size range from a basic pattern. This can be done manually or with CAD programs.
- **SHIPPERS & DISTRIBUTORS**—Those who deliver goods from the manufacturer to the buyers.

Specific production services assist in various phases of manufacturing. As a garment manufacturer, you will use all of them either consistently or occasionally. Many sewing contractors also provide in-house cutting, buttonhole/button-sew and snap-setting services. Sometimes contractors who specialize in a specific process offer a better price than a general sewing contractor. In costing your piece price, factor in the time and money involved in transporting the goods from one contractor to another for a specialized versus an in-house service.

Specific Production Services

- **(FABRIC) CONVERTERS**—People who oversee and/or perform the change of plain fabrics and greige goods into finished goods through any process applied or done to the fabric such as printing, water-proofing, stone washing or dyeing.
- **(FABRIC) DYE HOUSES**—Plants where fabric or piece goods are dyed.
- **SCREEN PRINTERS**—Plants where design is printed on fabric or piece goods (e.g., T-shirts).
- **CUTTING CONTRACTORS**—Companies or individuals who, at predetermined prices, cut yardage into pattern pieces by using scissors, rotary cutters (electric and hand), fabric saws or laser cutters.
- **SEWING CONTRACTORS**—Companies or individuals who sew work on a large scale according to contractual agreement at a predetermined price.
- **EMBROIDERERS**—Contractors who embroider apparel or sewn products at predetermined prices, usually using computer-driven embroidering sewing machines.

- **BUTTONHOLE/BUTTON-SEW SERVICES**—Contractors who sew buttonholes and buttons at predetermined prices using specialized sewing machines.
- **SNAP SETTERS**—Contractors who set snaps at predetermined prices using specialized machinery.

Regional associations, source books and information services will provide you with sources of these services. If you have worked in the garment industry, you will have some knowledge of who does what in your area or nationally. If not, you can start by looking in the Yellow Pages or, better yet, the Business to Business Yellow Pages for your area. Also check online. Ask anyone you can think of who might be familiar with names of people providing various services. This information is a closely guarded trade secret among manufacturers even though all of you may be using the same people for the same services at the same time.

Once you start talking to sewing contractors, for instance, and are in the "loop," the information is easier to come by. If one sewing contractor is too busy or does not have the right equipment or does not work with the delicate fabrics you are using, for example, then ask her for a referral. She will know what you need and probably be able to steer you in a good direction and save you much time and effort in your search. Always ask to see the work these contractors produce: Look at what is being sewn when you are in the sew shop or being printed at the screen printers. Ask for the names and phone numbers of some clients. Ask the clients about the sew shop's reliability, the timeliness of its delivery and the number of sewn items that did not meet quality control standards. These factors are as important as getting a good price per piece for the work.

Because of the recent federal crackdown on sweatshops, it is essential for all garment manufacturers to be licensed according to each state's requirements. If a sewing shop is "busted," everyone involved is held equally liable: the contractor, subcontractors and manufacturers whose goods are being sewn in the shop. Ask to see the appropriate state license. To save yourself headaches use properly licensed contractors.

See "Apparel Industry Contractor Agreement" on page 126.

Try out a production sewer or sewing contractor. If you can give her more than one piece (completed item, not pattern piece) to sew, she can provide you with a far more accurate piece price. The contractor needs to know that you intend to work with her in developing the product and establishing a price. Limit your comparison shopping.

Patternmakers, graders, sample sewers, production sewers and sewing contractors generally base their prices on an hourly rate. Ask them what their hourly rate is. You will then know how long they think it will take to do your job—whether it is the piece price for sewing a shirt together or the price to grade an elaborate dress pattern into five other sizes. Once you work consistently with sewers and you are used to each other's methods and the process, you both will be able to estimate the cost per piece easily. Eventually, you will tell them what you will pay per piece; this is what is expected of you. Negotiations will follow. Converters, dyers, screen printers, embroiderers, snap setters and buttonhole/button-sew shops will usually have set piece prices or will be able to quote you a price without costing your job specifically.

Manufacturers—large and small—must be able to evaluate the quality of the work they are paying for, the timeliness of its delivery and the general organization and efficiency of the production sewing and cutting contractors. A number of standard quality control (QC) measuring systems are commonly used in the industry: JCPenney, STR, Dayton-Hudson, ISO 9000.

These systems use quantifiable measures to evaluate overall factory efficiency and the quality of specific garment production runs. To produce usable information, they rely heavily on factory inspections, inventories of equipment and operations performed and in-line inspections. These measuring tools can provide you with some invaluable information about a contractor's performance history.

Generally, these systems are used by individual manufacturers

- to make an overall evaluation of a sewing contractor/factory by identifying and measuring the services provided, communications skills, organization, documentation of work and handling of raw materials.

- to measure QC of a specific production run by a specific contractor by quantifying inspection data and verifying costing procedures.

Ask cutting and sewing contractors under consideration to give you the names of their manufacturing clients who have used the evaluation tools discussed above. The manufacturers are the ones who hold the evaluation information. Then, contact them as references and ask them if they have any evaluation information about the specific contractor.

You can also ask contractors if they have any recent or current factory evaluations or quality control reports you can look at. Unless you are a paying customer or a prospective large customer the factory management is not likely to allow you to evaluate the factory or work in progress. As mentioned, you can ask to see samples of their work as it comes through the production line. As your production quantity increases, you will have more clout when interviewing new contractors.

Use the *Contractor Profile and Evaluation Form (page 129)* as a guide when you begin to search out contractors and evaluate their services for your product. Remember, you may need different contractors for different services. Keep all the information in a binder and update it annually.

 Tips for Interviewing and Using Services

- Ask all the questions you can think of to educate yourself. The more you know and the sooner you know it, the better businessperson you will be in this (or any) field.
- Always have several people or companies to work with in each area so that you have options and backups. It may take years to develop your network of service people and companies.
- If an estimated price does not seem right to you, discuss it with the provider of the service. Maybe there is miscommunication about what you want done or what they think you want done; ask about ways to lower costs.

Garment Manufacturer's License and Registration

Many states require garment-manufacturing licenses. Those states with the biggest garment industries and largest immigrant populations have the strictest regulations: California, Florida and New York. The purpose of the license and the regulations is to protect minority labor at risk. Some of the laws are outdated and some are still very important. The amount of federal enforcement by the Wage and Hour Division of the Department of Labor is directly related to the degree of state regulation of garment manufacturing.

For example, California State Law AB633 recently redefined who must obtain a **Garment Registration Certificate** to include any garment-manufacturing entity. In order to raise more money for enforcement of existing labor laws specific to the garment industry, fees for the certificate have been raised significantly. AB633 also provides some limited liability for manufacturers to cover the lost wages for employees of a contractor (used by the manufacturer) who goes out of business without paying workers. Workers can file a complaint with the Labor Commissioner for lost wages in these circumstances. If a company does no stateside cutting and sewing of samples or production but only designs and imports the finished product, it does not need a certificate. An application must be filled out *exactly*, a simple test—mainly on labor law—taken and a fee paid annually. Regulation and enforcement in California are very strict, probably the toughest in the country. (*See "Contractor's Certification of Compliance With Wage and Hour Laws" on page 128.*)

It is illegal to manufacture garments and accessories in the home in California.

Sew shops in homes are a very important focus of labor-law-enforcement agencies. Near major production sewing areas, many formerly employed production sewers have a machine or two in a room at home where they do production work for small local manufacturers as freelance contractors. They may need or want to work at home to care for children or elderly parents, and their working conditions may be optimal. Unfortunately, federal law (with a few exceptions for hats and gloves) and about ten states' laws prohibit or strictly control sewing work done in the home. Many more states require home workers to obtain permits or licenses. These homeworkers are not really the focus of the existing laws but by definition they are in violation of the laws. Keeping a low profile protects many of them from exposure and prosecution. The targets of the home-sewing laws are illegal sweatshops employing many workers, who work long hours in very poor and/or dangerous working conditions and are paid less than the minimum wage—and certainly no higher wages for overtime. Often, children are working under these same poor conditions. Many times, people are doing production sewing in the same rooms in which they eat and sleep.

"I'm licensed in New York, California and Florida."

Contractors vs. In-House Production

	Contractors	In-House Production
Labor	• They hire, lay off, do payroll, pay taxes and benefits. • They have greater access to additional trained workers as needed and can be responsive to seasonal demands. • They can be used to supplement in-house production time as needed. Contractors will undoubtedly have the same seasons of business and slack as you do, so you need to have a well-established relationship, one that is profitable to them, if you want them to be available to you upon demand.	• You hire, lay off, do payroll, pay taxes and benefits. • You will need a backup source of skilled labor to meet seasonal demands. All of your labor may be part-time/temporary or you may have some permanent/full-time help that you use to supplement your labor force as necessary.
Overhead	• It is included in their price to you.	• You must include it as part of your costs, in addition to the wages and benefits you pay your employees.
Control of Product	• You are paying them to produce according to your specifications and instructions. You are not present to oversee every step.	• You have responsibility for and total control of your production and the end product.
Cost	• Their piece price will be more than your in-house piece price, because their price includes overhead and profit.	• Your piece price will be derived from the direct costs of production—materials and labor—*plus* the overhead, labor benefits and payroll taxes you pay.
Hassles	• You are not the only customer using the contractor's services; sometimes you cannot get your work done when you want it done. • It is necessary to constantly spot-check the production. • You must pickup and deliver materials and cut and sewn goods.	• You deal with all human resource issues. • You must purchase or lease and maintain equipment. Someone must oversee work you are paying for.
Ease	• The contractor deals with labor and overhead issues.	• No delivery and pickup of cut and sewn pieces. • Changes in production are easy to accommodate, as is fast turnaround on samples or other orders/items.

CHAPTER 4: COSTING

You have made those first few samples of your design idea and received lots of positive feedback. You have found sources for fabric, pattern and sample making and maybe even production. Now it is time to go back to your market analysis and see what the going rate is for products like yours. If your design will be produced in a costlier fabrication, is there a market for it? That is a question that sometimes can be answered by looking at what is already on the market and sometimes only by putting that costlier version out there. It's "taking a gamble" time again. Making a few samples to take on a road-sales trip or to a trade show can be an inexpensive investment to see if that dream version will fly. But making a full set of samples for all your reps is not an inexpensive test.

Initial Costing Based on Time and Material

In this first round of establishing a price for your dream design you will calculate your initial costs by using data on the cost of producing **one** *item, not ten or twenty.* This initial costing is done before you know how many you will actually make when you are in production. So at this stage, all costs are projections. Once you are in production you will refine and finalize your costs relative to production in quantity.

Materials and Trim

Remember to use wholesale costs; this information should be on your Fabric/Trim Spec Sheets. Usually they are half of full retail costs, with some notable exceptions: Quantity purchases of zippers will cost 25¢ to 55¢ each wholesale, not the $1.85 or $2.00 you pay at a fabric store. Six thousand-yard cones of thread will cost $5 or $6, not $1.50 for 300 yards. Buttons are also an exception. If you purchase fabric or trim at a *discount* retail store you cannot use the prices as accurate guides to true retail or wholesale costs. Part of costing is finding the price of every piece of fabric, trim and thread used in *one* garment, accessory or sewn product.

- When calculating the amount of fabric each garment uses, be sure to include the amount of lining and interfacing, if needed.
- Include in the fabric costs the costs of having the goods (fabric and trim) shipped to you. If the cost of shipping fabric is $2 for ten yards, then the cost of shipping per yard is $2 divided by ten (yards) or 20¢ per yard.

Cutting and Sewing Labor

If you are using a cutter, production sewer or sewing contractor, she will give you a piece price—the price to cut and/or sew one garment, accessory or sewn product. All contractors have an hourly rate on which they base their piece prices depending on the complexity of each garment, the number of production steps involved and the sewing time. For example, rates will be calculated by specific operations, seam lengths and the amount of time each of these operations takes. Domestic contractor rates typically range from $6 to $10 per hour.

Production sewers using production equipment will sew approximately two to three times faster than you do on a home machine. Also, sew shops have many different machines for specific tasks. Consequently, the job will be done quickly and more easily and efficiently in a production sew shop—either in-house or at a contractor's. If you use a contractor, you will be paying for all his equipment as part of the overhead that is calculated into the hourly rate on which piece prices are based. If you have an in-house factory, you must include the cost of purchasing or leasing the equipment, as well as maintaining it, in your overhead. (Overhead includes rent, utilities, office expense, and so on.)

- When having samples sewn, you will be charged the price for **sewing samples**. Ask the contractor the estimated **production sewing price** of the same item. Sewing samples can cost two to three times the price of production sewing.
- Have the contractor break down the piece price by operation: for example, setting the sleeve, setting the zipper, sewing the trim, edge stitching the collar. With this information you can see where you can save money by simplifying construction.

If you are cutting and sewing your own samples, use the following steps to establish a piece price:

- When you start to cut or sew, plug in a clock set to exactly twelve o'clock, or start a stop watch. Unplug the clock or stop the stopwatch for any interruptions or breaks. Start the clock or stopwatch when you get back to cutting or sewing.

- Use the local standard hourly rate for a production sewer; rates differ throughout the country.

" I don't see it selling at that price."

Cost Sheets

Cost Sheets contain all the information about the cost of the style you are expecting to produce. As *first* cost sheets, they become the basis of all calculations for that style; once in production, a new sheet indicates *final* cost. Use a separate sheet for each style you are considering manufacturing for your current line. Keep them together in a notebook (with your Fabric/Trim Spec Sheets and Initial Design Spec Sheets). The following information must be included on each sheet.

- style name
- style number
- fabric costs
- trim costs
- cutting costs
- sewing costs

- packaging costs
- other costs
- first cost
- wholesale cost
- suggested retail cost

See "Cost Sheet" on page 132.

Costing Terminology

- ### FIRST COST

The total of all your direct costs of producing the item is your first cost.

Material + Labor = First Cost

- ### WHOLESALE COST

As a rule the first cost is doubled to arrive at the wholesale cost so that you cover your fixed costs (overhead) and selling expenses and create a profit. Marking up by doubling is called "keystoning."

First Cost x Markup = Wholesale Cost

- ### RETAIL PRICE

In establishing their retail prices, many retailers use the same keystoning formula for markup to cover their fixed costs (overhead) and selling expenses and to create a profit.

Wholesale Cost x Markup = Retail Price

If you will be selling your own goods at fairs or through your own catalog or mailing, your selling price should be halfway between the wholesale and the retail price. That pricing will help you cover your selling costs.

If your retail price is out of line with the going retail price, you will have to decide what you need to change in your first cost and how you will make those changes and still keep the integrity of your product design. Make sure that the cost of each style offered in a grouping makes sense with the costs of other styles in the grouping.

Tips for Costing

- Use the middle size of your size range for costing and estimating fabric needs.
- Date your cost sheet and each revision so that you have a record and history of your costing process.
- Make a cost sheet for each fabrication of a design: cost differences between fabrics will affect your total costs.
- Cost a style at one price for all colors.
- Cost a style at one price for all sizes unless your material and labor costs are substantially different in the smallest or largest sizes.
- Do not undercost or underprice your product or you will go out of business. You must cover your expenses and make a profit to succeed.

• Most, but not all, people in the industry use the keystone method of pricing: your sales price equals double your costs. But you can (legally) sell your product wholesale to many retail outlets, who will determine, by whatever method, the *retail* price at which they will actually sell it.

Chapter 5: Sales and Promotion Tools for Selling Your Product

Selling Seasons and Marketing Calendar

Follow the selling seasons as defined below. More importantly, pay attention to the fact that these days goods are sold much closer to the actual delivery dates than they were in the traditional calendar. E-commerce, catalogs and traditional brick-and-mortar (physical store) companies must all adhere to the same faster-paced schedule. In addition, catalogs need samples for photography earlier than traditional market dates and seasonal trade shows. They also want your product in their house when their catalog is dropped (mailed). Online retailers change their selling inventory frequently and quickly. Your response to their demand must be just about immediate. Brick-and-mortar establishments also work on a shorter turnaround time from sales to product in-house ready to ship, as well as changing inventory frequently.

SEASON	T	DD	T	DD	T	DD	T	DD	T	DD
FALL	1.1-2.28	1.1-6.30	2.15	2.15-7.15	3.15	3.15-7.31	5.1-7.15	5.1-8.15	6.30-9.30	6.30-10.15
HOLIDAY/ RESORT	4.1-5.31	4.1-9:30	5.15	5.15-10.15	6.1-8.15	6.1-10.15	8.1-10.1	8.1-11.15	10.1-12.15	10.15-1.30
SPRING	7.5-8.31	7.1-12.30	8.15	8.15-1.15	9.1-11.1	9.1-1.15	11.1-1.15	11-2.15	1.30-3.31	1.30-4.30
SUMMER	11.1-12.15	11.1-4.30	11.15	11.15-4.15	1.1-1.31	1.1-5.15	2.15-4.15	2.15-6.1	4.15-5.31	4.15-6.15

T = Traditional Calendar   **DD** = Dynamic Design   **Numbers** represent dates: 5.1 = May 1

Theoretically, buyers have "open to buy" money allocated for orders at these calendar times, and this is when you want to have your goods in their faces. **Dynamic Delivery** is the order of the day, and you, as a micro-enterprise, are well equipped to provide it. Basically, the sales tools discussed below stay the same no matter who is selling the line. Therefore, you want to develop a set of selling tools that are usable by everyone, are complete in and of themselves and can be combined easily and smoothly with other tools in a variety of selling situations.

Line Sheets

Line sheets come in many forms and provide information about your product. Any person selling your line will use them to answer questions about your products. They can be handed out in showrooms, at trade shows or on market days, used in direct mail sales and sent in response to inquiries. A line sheet can also be an order form that contains all the necessary information or an order form on one side and a line sheet on the other. There can be one sheet per product or many products per sheet. Generally, a line sheet is developed for a specific selling season, such as Spring or Fall. What is available to sell on that line sheet may also have a specific delivery period. In the case of items that are sold year-round, indicate turnaround time from order to delivery—"Allow six weeks for delivery," for example.

Develop the Line Sheet from information on your Initial Design Spec Sheets. Line Sheets should always include the following information:

- company name, address, phone, fax, e-mail and website information
- style names
- style numbers
- sketch or photo of each style
- short verbal description of items
- fiber content of bodies and trim
- colors and fabrications
- sizes

- prices
- country of manufacture/origin of fabric
- effective date(s) of line sheet
- delivery dates
- minimum orders
- sales terms
- additional information to clarify or explain the above data, e.g., "infant" size fits 3-6 months

Sample Line Sheet

COZY TOPS

COZY TOPS
1000 Main Street
Any Town, CA 00000-0000
800-000-0000 Fax 800-100-0000
www.cozytops.com

Season: Spring 2201
Delivery: 1/30-3/30
Minimum Order: $200

Reversible Baseball Hat
Style # 10

COST: $9.00

SIZES:

Small	0-6 months
Medium	6-12 months
Large	12-24 months
Preschool	2-4 years

Our adorable 100% cotton hat is comfortable and cool. There is a surprise color inside each brim! This is a year-round favorite for all children on the go!

COLORS:
100 Spring Fever
130 Dots
50 Stripes
10 White/logo embroidery
20 Black/logo embroidery

Back Flap Hat
Style # 12

COST: $11.00

SIZES:

Small	0-6 months
Medium	6-12 months
Large	12-24 months
Preschool	2-4 years

This hat is not only colorful and cute but also a great sun protector. The extended brim and back flap provide your children the sun protection they need in 100% cotton fabric

COLORS:
100 Spring Fever
130 Dots
150 Stripes
10 White/logo embroidery
20 Black/logo embroidery

All first orders are C.O.D. With credit approval reorders will be NET 30.
Any returns must be made within 10 days of receipt and with approval of our office.
5% discount on all prepaid orders.
A late charge of 1.5% per month is applied on all past-due accounts.
Special orders and private label available on request.

Cozy Tops   1000 Main Street   Any Town, CA   00000-0000   TEL 800-000-0000   FAX 800-100-0000

Samples for Selling Purposes

Samples for selling purposes are used by any person selling your line—you, your sales reps or other salespeople in showrooms, at trade shows, on market days and on the road. Samples are your front line of selling tools: they show exactly what the buyer is ordering and what will be shipped. Not only should your samples be perfect, they must accurately represent what you are actually producing and shipping. Samples for selling purposes should

- include one of each style you are selling

- be of the best materials

- be perfectly sewn

- be the most attractive of the color ways you are offering

- be the size that best shows off the design of the item

- have a swatch card of other colors, prints or fabrics in which this item will be produced

- have a sample tag which lists fabric content, sizes, colors offered and price points

Hangtags for samples provide all the information about a specific style to a buyer writing an order. Use tags of heavy card stock which can be plastic-coated after printing (by hand or machine) so they stand up well to repeated handling.

Hangtags should be secured to a garment in a location that does not take away from the aesthetics of the item, such as a center back seam or underarm. Hangtags can be attached by safety pins, string, yarn, ribbon or by a plastic swift tab—just like the ones on garments you buy at a retail store. The information on hangtags for samples should include

- your logo
- company name and address
- style name

- style number
- size range

- color range
- fiber content
- country of manufacture and country of origin of fabric

- price point (the selling price)
- minimums per style

There should be a separate swatch card of available fabrications—this can save you fabric and production costs in sample making by allowing customers to see the full range of colors and fabrics.

COZY TOPS

Style:	10 Reversible Baseball Hat
Colors:	100 spring fever
	130 dots
	150 stripes
	10 white/logo embroidery
	20 black/logo embroidery
Sizes:	S, M, L, PS
Delivery:	1/30-3/30
Fiber:	100% Cotton
Cost:	$9.00

(Print your company logo here)

COZY TOPS
1000 Main Street
Any Town, CA. 00000-0000
800-000-0000
800-100-0000 Fax

Sales Displays

Sales displays for showrooms, road sales or other purposes should present your products in their best light. Display forms should be in excellent condition. Samples of your products should be perfect examples of the quality and style of what you manufacture. Show off your goods to their best advantage in a professional manner. Use quality bags and cases and upscale hangers, not ones from the cleaners. Sales display items include the following:

- mannequins or forms in showrooms
- hangers in showrooms and for road sales
- other display items appropriate to displaying your product: heads for hats, trays for jewelry, etc.

"Now that will catch someone's eye!"

Trade Show Displays

Trade show displays can be self-decorated or professionally decorated/dressed. It is quite possible to create an exciting display on your own at no great expense. Use your imagination—the same one that came up with these great design ideas that you are trying to manufacture and sell. You can use anything that best sets off your product, including things that you already own. Enlarged and mounted photos of your product, modeled or displayed at its best, are always great sales tools. A professional decorator/dresser will do a slick job; it will look good. It will be costly.

Signage

Signage, in a basic form, is always provided by the trade show organizers. If you will be doing shows regularly, it is worth investing in a professionally made sign that will be of a higher quality and should draw more attention to your booth.

Free Publicity

Trade and other magazines are always looking for editorial copy—the written material on the page that is not advertising. Of course, they want the latest style, the newest look, the cleverest gimmick. At trade shows, editors, writers and other magazine representatives will be looking for all of the above. If they have an interest in photographing your product, they will ask for samples for that purpose. Usually they want to pick them up on the spot. This is not always practical, since your samples may be the only one(s) of a particular style that you have with you for selling purposes. If that is the case, ask the magazine person to come back near the end of the show, when sales are generally slow and the absence of a display item or sample is not that critical. But if you have extras, you can provide them when asked. Be sure to fill out an invoice that indicates exactly what you are giving and to whom and include it with the samples. Be sure to get a business card from the person requesting the sample. Sometimes, in the course of events, your samples will get lost or destroyed, so indicate the price of the items on the invoice and write across the invoice and/or in the terms box: "No Charge If Returned in Good Condition." This way your potential losses are indicated upfront. There should be no problem in being reimbursed if loss or destruction of your samples occurs. As mentioned earlier, you need extra samples for times like this. If you are asked to ship samples overnight to a publication, ask them for their Fed Ex or other shipping number. They should and will pay the charges for the express shipping. Also, the new products editor of a magazine always welcomes press releases about new products. It is free copy, already written, which they can and will use in the new products section of the magazine. You get exposure of your product. Another win-win scenario for free publicity.

Once your photos appear in the magazine, hopefully on the cover, the magazine will usually send you tear sheets of the pages and/or copies of the magazine. They may even send you a mounted cover, if you are fortunate enough to get your product on the cover. If they do not offer the tear sheets or copies, be sure to ask them for what you want. Use all of this for free publicity, just as they have used your product as grist for the mill of editorial coverage. Keep a portfolio of your product's publicity in a binder with clear plastic sheets. Enlarge a photo and mount it on foam-core board and use it in your display.

Advertising

Advertising exposes many people to your product via a variety of media. Any advertising you do as a micro-enterprise selling at wholesale will be to retail stores and catalogs via trade magazines. These ads, which are costly, can be placed in issues that are distributed free at trade shows; often the relevant edition of a trade magazine and the show directory will be one and the same publication. Sometimes there are less expensive ways of advertising within a publication, such as a new-product page or directory. This exposure will undoubtedly give you more visibility and should bring more people to your booth to see your product and buy it.

As your business grows, you may want to increase your brand-name recognition by advertising to the general public in all the ways our culture offers us: the Internet, TV, radio, magazines, newspapers, direct mailings, etc. You can plan your advertising campaign to include promotions at retailers throughout your targeted area. Usually, getting your company name and product in the public's consciousness is a serious expense. Try for as much free publicity as possible and use all the promotional materials that free publicity generates.

Direct and Indirect Sales

At first you may sell to friends and family by explaining to them that "this" is your product. Then you might do some craft/street fairs or designer showcase shows. Next, you decide to sell wholesale through store buyers. At this point, you are using sales samples to sell products for future delivery. You are no longer selling stock on hand at the point of sale. Instead, you will be writing orders at the point of sale, manufacturing the goods, shipping them and then getting paid. This step brings both the opportunity to make more money and the frustration of not receiving that money until 14 to 120 days after delivery—from C.O.D. to very late payment, a hair away from collections.

All the selling that you personally do provides you with invaluable feedback. Those first few sales to friends and family boost your ego; the sales at street or craft fairs build your confidence and provide you with feedback from your public. Your public will let you know what they like, what they find missing and wish they could have and what is good or bad about your product. It is important to listen to and analyze their feedback. If people do not like a product, they will not buy it; if they tell you how to make your product into something they would like, listen carefully! In the midst of this public opinion and feedback you must adhere to your own vision and sense of aesthetic. It can be a difficult call sometimes.

After a road trip or two and a trade show or two you will have a fairly clear sense of how you and your product fit into the marketplace. You will have a working relationship with those vendors who retail to your target market. You will experience the competition in action. If you sell online you will have sales data and customer response to factor into the equation. You will have begun the process of fine-tuning your product to meet consumer demands. All of this information makes you a better designer, manufacturer and salesperson. You will be ready to talk knowledgeably to sales reps about your product and your target market. You will be in an excellent position to negotiate a good deal because of your knowledge. Also, the longer you are at it, the better businessperson you will become.

If you are truly committed to making a success of your design-based business, you must make the quantum leap from individual retail sales and small wholesale sales at local venues to nation-wide exposure in wholesale marketing venues and/or retail online venues for your product. There is no other way to be seen and make it happen.

Secure Websites

All selling online must be done through secure websites. Many companies, including ISPs (Internet Service Providers), offer these services. If people feel secure about their credit card information not being stolen, they are more likely to buy at the site.

Consignment Sales

You will receive approximately 50 percent of the retail price when your goods placed on consignment are sold. Payment can be immediate or in thirty days. Prices for goods placed on consignment are usually reduced after a given amount of time, so your half of the retail sales price will be less. Goods often get shopworn while on consignment; if they are returned to you unsold they will probably be in unsalable condition. If all the goods in a store are on consignment, salespeople will give them equal attention. But if your consignment goods are among goods that the shop has already bought and paid for then it is realistic to expect that salespeople will try to sell those already-paid-for goods first.

Road Sales

- **Locating Prospects to Visit**

  - Pick your target areas by demographics, previous experience, word of mouth, appropriate Yellow Pages at the library—look at the ads.

  - Be selective about the stores you visit. Do not try to sell inexpensive junior sportswear to a store that carries expensive art-to-wear for an over-forty market.

  - Make sure the look of your line works in the store. Preview: do a drive-by and a commando-raid visit to scope out the store as an appropriate prospect, to see if your line fits. Get a business card and the name of the buyer/owner. Then the next day you can say: "I'd like to show you my line. I was in your store yesterday and I know my line works with the look of your store"— or something similar.

    and/or

  - Preview by having telephone conversations and faxing or mailing your sales materials.

  - *Never Make Cold Calls*—it is unprofessional and is disrespectful of both you and the buyer.

- **Setting Up Sales Appointments**

  - Make a list of your prospects in a geographic area.

  - Figure on three or, at most, four sales calls in a day—that is about all you will have time for if you are going from town to town or around a big city.

  - Use a map to plot and plan your ideal route.

  - Plan your appointments on Monday, Tuesday, Wednesday, maybe Thursday. Friday, Saturday and Sunday are the busiest selling days for most retail stores and they are selling, not buying, on those days.

  - Call your prospects to set up appointments with the store owner or person responsible for buying, not a salesclerk.

  - Store owners are aware of the vagaries of sales trips and most will be adaptable to your scheduling needs.

- **Getting There**

  - Get directions to the store, as needed.

  - Allow sufficient time between appointments.

- **Proper In-Store Behavior**
  - Often the store owner/buyer will be the only person in the store looking at your line *and* serving customers; *wait patiently* while the buyer takes care of customers and makes sales. Remember that the store owner's primary interest is making sales, which will take precedence over looking at your line.

  - Store owners will gladly let you use their restroom facilities.

  - If you need to make a phone call, use a cellular phone or pay phone.

- **Maximizing *Your* Presence in Their Territory**
  - Showing your line out of a sample case or on the floor or in limited space—not under optimal circumstances—can be a challenge.

  - Carry your goods in nice-looking carrying cases—not plastic bags and metal hangers from the cleaners.

  - The goods in your carrying cases should be easy to access.

  - Keep all versions of a style or a line together.

  - Make it easy for yourself to show your line out of bags and cases.

Selling Tips

- "Let me show you the line."
- "This is/these are our bestseller(s)."
- Find what other lines the store sells—to encourage conversation and to see if and how your line fits in.
- Share the information you have about how your product sells; inform and guide your buyers.
- If your line is new to the store or the store itself is new, consider the advantages of flexibility regarding minimums. Encourage and help them to try your product. Remember, they are attracted enough by it to walk into your booth or showroom in the first place.
- Never interfere with a sale in progress at a showroom, in a sales booth or in a store on the road. If you and a fellow exhibitor are talking when a potential customer appears for your fellow exhibitor, quietly remove yourself from the scene. If you are selling in a store and your customer has a retail sale to make, wait quietly until your customer is available to you.

- If a sales order will not fly—for whatever reason—call the customer yourself to straighten out the problem. More than likely you will increase the size of the order with that phone call. Personal interest in doing it right pays dividends.

Trade Shows

Your product is developed. Sample production is complete and your sales materials are finished. Everything is looking good. You want more exposure than local selling trips provide. You are ready to put your product on display for the world to see. Let the orders begin! And remember that this next step in the process is a costly one.

Plan ahead. Get information about the shows you are interested in well ahead of the Spring and Fall shows. Previous/repeat exhibitors get first pick of the spaces, and shows can sell out quickly. Floor plans and price lists are available six months ahead of the show dates. Also remember to ask for and follow union rules that control setup and break-down procedures and about the costs of trade shows.

See "U.S. Regional Apparel Markets and Marts" on page 117.

 Tips on Selecting Trade Shows

- Selling season—Trade shows occur during the official selling seasons. (*See "Selling Seasons and Marketing Calendar" on page 59.*)
- Target market—If you are selling kids' hats, you will want to do a kids show.
- Dates—If you sell a spring product, you will want to do a Spring show, *which occurs in the fall.*
- Quality of venue—Some shows have better reputations and attract a better crowd of buyers than other shows. Ask around.
- Geographical location—If you want to tap the East Coast market, attend a trade show on the East Coast. If you want to keep travel costs down, attend a show close to home. Also, remember that regional tastes vary.
- Costs—They will be high. The basic booth or showroom may cost from $1,200 to $3,000, depending on the size of your booth and the specific trade show. And there are plenty of extras. *See next page.*

What Your Show Costs Generally Cover

- Listing in the show directory (usually by company name, by booth number and by category)

- Space/booth/showroom

- Carpeting

- Side and back walls/curtains

- Chairs

- Tables (they are bare, ugly and best covered with drapes)

- Cartage of your display between the loading dock and booth at the start and finish of the show

- Cardboard sign

- Storage of valuables during the show

- Racks

- Shelves

- Risers—wooden frames to create display

Extras You Generally Pay For

- Airfare

- Room, board and entertainment

- Ground transportation

- Shipping your display items to and from the show

- Table drapes

- Lights or electricity for your own lights

- Storage of display items before and after the show

- Decorating your booth or showroom: Do it yourself (cost of materials); hire a decorator (labor and materials)

Advantages That Offset/Outweigh Costs

- Orders

- Exposure

- Mailing list—Get a business card every time you hand out a line sheet; these names become your mailing list and these people will return to buy eventually. Keep your name in prospects' minds with postcard mailings before each trade show.

- Contacts

- Future orders

- Gaining invaluable information from fellow exhibitors—through both observation and casual conversation

See "Check List For Trade Shows" on page 133.

Credit Cards

The use of credit cards by manufacturers to purchase materials and supplies and by retailers to pay for ordered goods has become very common. Their use assures the seller of receiving payment and allows the buyer additional time to pay the bill and obtain pre-approved credit if needed. By short-circuiting the cash-flow dramas of garment manufacturing, the use of credit cards reduces the need for factors (financial service companies), which are becoming a rare breed.

How to Write an Order

The following is basic information for writing an order anywhere, anytime. Orders can be written on blank ready-made multicopy forms available at stationery stores. They should have three or four parts. You give one to the buyer and keep the other parts for your production, tracking and order-packing functions. You can use your company's rubber stamp at the top of the pages to identify your business. Eventually, you may wish to have your own forms printed that include specifics important to your product and how you do business. Photocopied or computer-generated single sheets will require the use of carbon paper. Write the order legibly using a ballpoint pen. If a buyer supplies you with a business card, make sure that all the information you need is there and current, including area code, zip code and the buyer's name.

Often, you will start an account on a C.O.D. (cash or cashier's check only) basis, especially when they want the order in a hurry and you have no time to check their credit. You can systematically advance to Net 30 as you continue to do business with them and they maintain good credit with you.

"Do you think this new style will sell better
at the North Pole or the South Pole?"

Sample Order Form

COZY TOPS
1000 Main Street
800-000-0000

F 800-100-0000

SALESPERSON: Kathy
PHONE: 888 000 0000
SHIP VIA: UPS

BILL TO: Small Things
2 State Street
Somewhere, USA 00000-0000

SHIP TO: Same

Order Date: 10-23-2020   Start Date: 12-01-2020   Cancel Date: 12-05-2020   Terms: Net 30

Style 10   Reversible Baseball Hat   100% Cotton

Fabrication	Small	Medium	Large	Pre-School	Quantity	Unit Cost	Total
100 Spg.Fvr	3	3	3	0	0	$8.00	$72.00
130 Dots							
150 Stripes		2	2	2	6	$8.00	$48.00
10 Wht/Logo							
20 Blk/Logo							

Style 12   Back Flap Hat   100% Cotton

Fabrication	Small	Medium	Large	Pre-School	Quantity	Unit Cost	Total
100 Spg.Fvr							
130 Dots	3	3	3	3	12	$10.00	$120.00
150 Stripes							
10 Wht/Logo							
20 Blk/Logo							

BUYER'S SIGNATURE_____

UNIT TOTAL   27
MERCHANDISE TOTAL $120.00
SHIPPING TOTAL
C.O.D.
TOTAL

Order-Form Information

The following information must be included on all orders that you write for your products..

- Your company Name, address, phone and fax numbers, email and website addresses

- Bill To and Ship To

  Include the store/company name and the buyer's name, address, phone and fax numbers and e-mail address. The Bill To and Ship To information may be the same of different

- Order Date

- P.O. #

- Salesperson

- Delivery/ Shipping Date—

  Be very accurate and clear about when the store wants to take delivery. Sometimes the shipping date is specified rather than the delivery date. It can take at least one week for goods to ship via ground transportation from coast to coast, for example. Whatever dates are decided upon, be absolutely sure to indicate on the order whether this date is a delivery date or a shipping date.

- Start Date—

  The first date of a window of time (November 15-November 30) during which an order is to be shipped/delivered.

- Cancel Date—

  Usually the last date of a window; if the order is not received by that date, the order is automatically canceled.

- Shipping Instructions—

  UPS, RPS, FedEx or USPS. Ground, 3-Day Select, 2nd Day, Next Day. Partial order shipping details.

- (Credit) Terms (of the sale)—

  See the Credit Terminology information below and the Samplepage 73 Order Form on page 73 for information important to order writing.

- Style Number/Name

- Color Number/Name

- Fabrication Number/Name

- Size or Prepacks

- Unit Cost—

  Cost per item.

- Line Cost—

  Unit cost times number of items ordered per line.

- Merchandise Total—

  Total of all line costs.

- Order Authorization

The following items should appear on the order form, although they will not be filled in until the item is shipped. They notify the customer that these charges may apply to the order.

- Shipping
- C.O.D. Charge
- Total

Behind which door is the order?

Sales Reps

Once you have some road sales trips and trade shows under your belt and have begun to know your way around the block, you will be ready to locate some sales reps to sell your product through-out the country (and world). No doubt you will want to reach all of your market all of the time—not just the generally regional and seasonal draw of most trade shows. In addition, your time is fully occupied by the many other parts of your business. The selling of your product in as many markets as possible will soon become something you alone cannot do. You want and need nationwide cov-erage by people whose full-time job is to sell your product (and others').

Sales representatives sell goods in permanent showrooms and/or go on the road. They focus on a specific area: women's bridge sportswear, or accessories, or infant/layette, for example, and they usually sell several different lines that work well together and do not compete with one another. Be sure to find out which other lines the rep sells and what they look like. Permanent showrooms for clothing reps in the larger cities are usually all located in the same building(s). For a commission 10 percent to 20 percent a sales rep will show your goods and write orders for you. Some reps, with showrooms in the largest cities, may also charge a monthly showroom fee. Sales reps can also sell your goods for you at their local trade shows; again, they will charge you a pro-rated-by-space booth

Credit Terminology

• Pro forma—	• Prepayment.
• C.O.D.: Cash On Delivery—	• Payment is due on delivery of goods either by check, cash or cashier's check.
• Net 30—	• Payment is due 30 days after you ship the goods. There is a gray area between the date you ship and the date the goods are received.
• 2%-10/Net 30—	• A 2% discount is given if bill is paid in full within ten days; otherwise full amount of bill due in 30 days.
• EOM—	• End Of Month. Regardless of ship/delivery date, all bills are due at the end of the month.
• Interest fees on balance due past Net 30—	• Generally 1½% per month or 18% per year.
• Credit check—	• Checking the credit of prospective accounts with their other suppliers or through credit-rating services.
• Credit history sheets—	• These forms, to be filled out by the buyer, storeowner or bookkeeper, should supply you with sufficient credit information so that you can decide whether or not to do business with the store and on what credit terms. Sometimes only paid-up vendors are listed, and therefore the information may have limited value.
• Credit-rating services—	• Firms that track the credit of businesses or individuals; an invaluable, though expensive, tool.
• Shipping policy—	• When you ship and what carrier you use.
• Return policy—	• Conditions under which you will accept returned goods.

fee, in addition to their commission. If and when you have your own booth at a trade show or mart, in addition to goods in your sales rep's booth, you will need to clarify which sales you will pay commission on. Your rep will want commission on all orders written for stores located in his territory. You may wish to pay commission only on orders from his existing customers that you write and/or orders that he actually writes. Be sure to clarify this before the show or when you initially establish your agreement. NEGOTIATE THE TERMS OF YOUR AGREEMENT.

fee, in addition to their commission. If and when you have your own booth at a trade show or mart, in addition to goods in your sales rep's booth, you need to clarify which sales you will pay com

Generally, showrooms are open during standard business hours; buyers can make appointments or just walk in. Showroom reps keep in contact with buyers as part of their daily sales routine to keep orders flowing.

Road reps regularly hit the road to sell their/your goods to established customers and also to check out new sales possibilities. When the rep is in the store, buyers can compare what the rep is selling with what is in stock and what is on order. This approach is particularly useful if your line is an accessory line. Road reps generally charge the same commission rates as showroom reps, trading off the expense of being on the road for the cost of a permanent showroom. Sales appointments are usually set up by the rep as she continually works the territory. Also, buyers can request a sales call.

How Do I Find a Sales Rep?

- Walk the nearest fashion trade center. When you find a showroom with which your line is compatible, in terms of both style and price points, get a business card. Then, call to set up an appointment to show them your line. Be sure to mention that you have seen their showroom and it looks as if your line belongs with their existing lines. NOTE WELL: *Never interfere with a sales transaction. Making a sale is the primary order of business in a salesroom (or at a trade show). Always set up an appointment ahead of time to show the rep your line.*

- At trade shows there are bulletin boards of "Reps Looking for Lines" or "Lines Looking for Reps." Also, sales reps often walk the show looking for new lines to rep. And you can walk the show looking for a sales rep to sell your line. Check out the booths set up by various sales reps; they are fairly obvious because of the large number of different lines sold in one booth.

- Talk to other manufacturers for referrals.

- Talk to store owners/buyers for referrals.

- Look in or advertise in (local) garment-business trade papers or magazines.

How Do I Find the <u>Right</u> Rep?

- Talk with other manufacturers the rep handles.

- Talk with buyers who buy from the rep.

- Patience and determination. Trial and error.

What Does the Sales Rep Look For?

- A product that will sell well and a product that works well with the rest of his lines.

- A manufacturer who reliably ships a quality product on time.

Remember...

- Both you and the sales rep want to make money from your collaboration.

- A sales rep is in the business of selling and will try to sell you himself also.

• Any successful relationship requires clear communication between/among all parties.

Samples for the Sales Rep

• You will need to provide your sales rep with a sample set of your line. If you have a road rep, the sample set needs to be easy to carry about. Or, if showroom space is limited, it may be that you provide one sample of each style and include swatch cards for all the fabrications.

• Also, sometimes sales reps will decide to show only certain items—your bestsellers, or what they deem their customers are most likely to be interested in. They may ask you for samples of just these items or may take a full sample line and show what they choose. Try your best to get them to show your entire line.

• Feedback is always most valuable. Listen to any suggestions they make *and then analyze* them carefully relative to what you already know about your product, your market and your competition.

Paperwork and Payment to and for the Sales Rep

The day you ship orders to a sales reps' accounts, you should also send a copy of the invoices for each of those shipments to the sales rep. The rep then knows the actual delivery dates, if any questions arise. The rep also knows when to contact that account for reorders. Reps like to know that complete orders are shipping on time; it is information that always makes them happy.

Only when you have received payment from the account do you pay the sales rep. This can be on a weekly or monthly or quarterly basis, as predetermined by you and the rep when you negotiate your agreement.

See "Sales Rep Agreement" on page 134.

"It's crafted of fine Tahitian wool by little old machines in the U.S.A."

CHAPTER 6: PRODUCING YOUR PRODUCT

How to Decide What and How Much to Manufacture

- **A. Total Your Orders Per Item**

At the end of a trade show, a selling season or each month, tally all of your orders by style, size and fabrication. This can be done by hand or quickly and efficiently by industry-specific computer software. If you ship monthly, you may want to tally monthly. If you ship within specific two-week windows, you will want to tally your orders at the end of a selling season in order to plan your production.

- PRODUCE a particular style or fabrication that is popular—you have many orders.
- DO NOT PRODUCE any style or color if very few of either are ordered.
- DO NOT PRODUCE only one style or size in a particular fabrication because you will not have sufficient use for the fabric to warrant buying and storing it as inventory. Or you may not meet minimum fabric orders.

You will not produce every style that you show. When you determine what you will and will not produce, immediately notify those customers who have ordered items that you have decided not to produce and offer them replacements in other styles. You want to hang on to these orders and these accounts; try your best to please them with what you do have to offer.

- **B. Calculate the Quantities of Fabric and Trim You Will Need to Produce These Items and Fill These Orders**

If one dress takes 2½ yards and you have orders for 500 red corduroy dresses, you will need 1,250 yards of red corduroy to make those dresses.

- **C. Order Approximately 125 percent of the Quantities Calculated in B (above) for Production of Reorders**

If you need 1,250 yards of red corduroy to fill orders in-house, then order 1,563+/- yards to cover orders already in-house, fabric flaws and cutting mistakes and to get a head start on expected reorders. Fabric comes in rolls or bolts of a given or approximate length or weight. Ask the fabric sales rep how many yards per roll—as a rule—and then order the number of rolls that comes closest to the yardage you need.

The Basic Steps in Manufacturing What You Have Sold

Review page 46, "Manufacturing Services" and "Garment Manufacturer's License and Registration" for tips on evaluating and selecting design and production services.

Grading Patterns

Grade only those patterns that you will actually produce; only incur the cost of grading if you will be using the graded pattern. So, if you need to produce all sizes and your sample pattern was in size 4, you now need to have patterns for all sizes. Patterns can be graded by hand or by using CAD. There are many software programs available for pattern grading, starting at about $1,500. You can contract out grading for a flat fee per size, usually about $25-$35 for a dress, for example, or by the hour.

Making Markers

For production, styles are generally cut in size ratio determined by how sizes sell: two of size 2, two of size 4, four of size 6, eight of size 8, eight of size 10, six of size 12, four of size 14. If you use a cutting service or contractor, they will make the marker (the paper layout for cutting pattern pieces) from your cut sheet (a list of the number of pieces or complete items per size). Cutters will often prepare the marker for a flat fee; the markers can be copied on a blueprint machine and you can use them repeatedly if your cut ratio remains the same, thus saving marker-making costs. You can make a marker yourself by using marker paper with an inch grid. Trace or blueprint your pattern pieces onto the arrangement that uses the fabric most efficiently.

Production Flow Chart

This chart plots the various options you have in manufacturing your product.

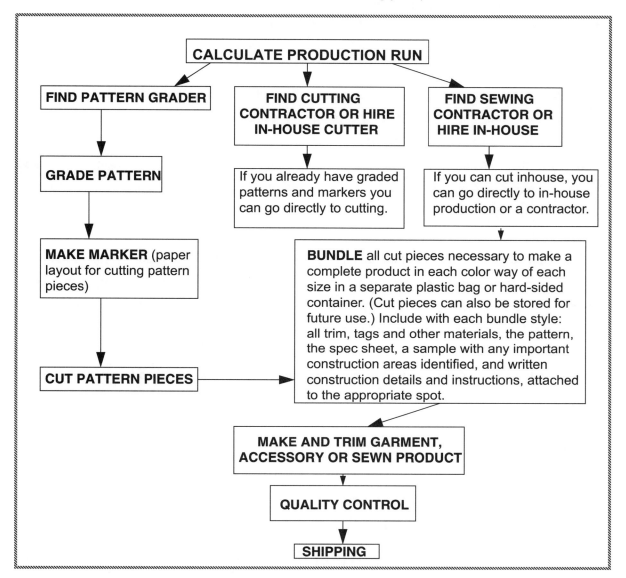

 Tips for Making a Marker and Laying Out a Cut

- **FABRICATIONS**: A thickness of up to six inches of various, but similar fabrics of the same width can be laid out and cut at the same time.
- **STYLES**: Pattern pieces of more than one style made of the *same fabrication* can be laid out and cut at the same time.

- **SIZES**: The *same size* in the *same or similar fabrics* in *different colors* can be cut at the same time.
- **DO NOT CUT KNITS AND WOVENS TOGETHER.**
- **CUT SHEERS BY THEMSELVES.**
- **DO NOT CUT PILE FABRICS WITH FABRICS WITH NO PILE.**

Cutting and Sewing

Cutting requires a smooth-surfaced, sturdy cutting table at least sixty inches wide and ten feet long for laying out fabric for cuts. It also requires electric fabric-cutting equipment—an electric straight-blade or electric rotary-blade cutting machine. If you use a contractor, establish the price prior to the start of cutting. Fabric must be shipped or delivered to them; cut pieces must be picked up from them. As when dealing with all contractors, you must keep close tabs on your goods: *make sure that you get the correct amount of cut pieces from the amount of yardage delivered to the contractor.*

Sewing requires a variety of industrial or power sewing machines. These can be purchased new or used, rented or leased with an option to buy. If you have an in-house factory, either get a service contract or have a good sewing-machine mechanic available. If you use a contractor, prices must be established prior to the start of production. Payment is at time of pickup; once you have an established relationship you may have up to fifteen days to pay. Contractors pay their help weekly for the work done that week. If the people who sew your goods get paid on time because the contractor has the money to pay them, they will be happy campers. This is a most desirable state for any people who work for you.

Mr.
Fashion Forward

© 1993, 1994 LEO CULLUM

Cut pieces, trim, tags, thread, and so on must be delivered to the contractor. Finished goods must be picked up from them. You must make sure that items are sewn to your specs (see Quality Control below) and that you receive all the pieces for which you are being charged.

Use a four-part cut-sew "ticket." You write down what you want cut and sewn and keep one copy. The cutter writes down what he actually cuts and keeps one copy; you pass the now two-part form on to the sewer, who writes down what she has actually sewn and keeps a copy. You now have the remaining copy, which shows how many you wanted cut and sewn and how many were actually cut and sewn. These are the numbers on which you base your payment: what you actually get. These figures allow you to see if, when and where losses or problems are occurring.

Purchase Order/Cut-Sew Tickets

Purchase Order/Cut-Sew Tickets contain all the information the contractor and you need to know about orders being delivered to them for production. Use one Purchase Order for each order you are delivering. Keep copies of all the P.O.s in a notebook with your Fabric/Trim Spec Sheets, Initial Design Spec Sheets, Cost Sheets, Quality Control Sheets and Production Spec Sheets. This form should provide the following:

- company name, address, telephone number, contact person
- delivery date (date due back to you or date finished—ready to be picked up.)
- piece price or other predetermined price for cutting, sewing or trimming goods
- number of items by style, size, color or fabrication

REMEMBER: In addition to all the materials necessary to complete the garment, bring the proto-type, patterns and spec sheet every time you are placing an order for a new cut or sew job.

See "Purchase Order/Cut-Sew Ticket" on page 135.

Quality Control

Whatever quality and "qualities" you are controlling must be specifically spelled out on your Production Spec Sheet and your Purchase Order/Cut-Sew Ticket. You should inspect for quality control frequently and throughout the production process, not just when the goods are finished. You do not want to spend money to continue production of items that are already not up to your standards. Continuous quality control will help you to correct problems before you are ready to ship the goods.

Quality Control Spec Sheets

These sheets identify the quality control elements of each style. Use one sheet for each style you are manufacturing. Keep your copies in a notebook with your Fabric/Trim Spec Sheets, Initial Design Spec Sheets, Cost Sheets, Production Spec Sheets and Purchase Order/Cut-Sew Tickets. The following items are typical of the information included on Quality Control Spec Sheets.

- number of stitches per inch
- fabric flaws
- production errors
- dirt or spots

- off sizes
- right side of fabric
- cleanliness
- other

See "Quality Control Sheet" on page 136.

Production Spec Sheets

These sheets detail each style *actually being produced* and are developed from your Initial Design Spec Sheets and Fabric Spec Sheets. When placing an order, you will give the contractor the Production Spec Sheet along with the Quality Control Sheet, Purchase Order/Cut-Sew Ticket, prototype and pattern. A copy of this spec sheet often stays attached to the pattern itself for easy reference. Use a separate sheet for each style being produced. Keep your copies together in a notebook with your Fabric/Trim Spec Sheets, Initial Design Spec Sheets, Cost Sheets, Purchase Order/Cut-Sew Tickets and Quality Control Sheets. The following information must be included on each sheet.

- company name, address, telephone number
- contact person
- date you deliver fabric to be cut
- date you deliver cut pieces to be sewn
- style number(s)
- style name(s)
- line drawing of product

- quantities of materials needed
- size
- color or fabrication
- suppliers
- fabric swatches
- specific instructions

See "Production Spec Sheet" on page 138.
See "Independent Contractor Agreement" on page 137.

"Yes, our business has grown
but we still love working at home!"

CHAPTER 7: PRODUCT DISTRIBUTION, MANAGEMENT AND PAYMENT

Tracking Orders

SKUs (Stock Keeping Units): Identification by Style, Size and Color or Fabrication

It is advisable to keep track of the production progress of every item in all orders. This can be done by using SKU numbers and industry-specific or other database software. Every style/size fabrication breakdown is assigned a specific number. Once an SKU item begins the production process, it should be entered in the database and its progress noted from step to step. This tracking allows you to keep accurate control of your product and ensures that you will meet delivery deadlines, barring the usual things that can and do go wrong.

Style Numbers and Names

You can achieve the same product-tracking capability by assigning each style a number and establishing other codes for color and size. Keep track of each style, size and color as it proceeds through production with handwritten methods; they still work well!

The important thing is to be able to identify where specific items necessary to fill specific orders by specific dates are in the production line at any given time. If a problem arises with a particular style, size, color item, you can make a decision on how to handle the problem. Also, it may be necessary to notify customers who have ordered a particular problem item of any delays or other setbacks.

Inventory Management

The first step is to control the packaging or boxes and/or the racks that are used to return your goods to you from the sewers. If you require that all goods be separated by style, size and fabrication, you will have an easy time putting goods into inventory storage areas or directly into shipping boxes for your customers. The sewers can easily do this separating because that is how the goods are sewn: by style, size and color. Give specific instructions on your Production Spec Sheets about whether finished goods are to be returned pressed and about how they should be packaged when returned to you.

You will need storage space for raw materials and completed goods—you want to be able to find what you need and find it in good condition! Dirty, light-faded, wrinkled, torn goods are not acceptable. Drawers, shelves, clothes racks—all covered to protect against dirt and light—are the order of the day. You will need a systematic way to pull items and pack them to fill orders.

- Tabulate all style/size/fabrication combinations that you need to fill all the orders that you are preparing for shipping at a given time.
- Then pull all the items: keep them separate by style/size/fabrication.
- Pack each order from those separate piles you created. You will need lots of space for this system to work well.

You will need to keep a tally of your inventory that will fluctuate as production runs come in-house and orders ship out. The use of comprehensive industry-specific software will automatically reduce your inventory numbers when you fill and ship orders. All you have to do is to remember to enter the data about the completed goods in the computer inventory when you get them in-house.

Supply Chain Management (SCM)

The use of computers and sophisticated software systems to handle multiple levels of product development and design, as well as sourcing, sales and marketing, production and distribution, streamlines operations within the company. SCM and similar systems, such as CPFR, address these complex interfaces so that all parts of the company, its suppliers and often its customers can have constant access to up-to-the-minute information about what is happening in each stage of the process.

UPC and EDI

The use of bar codes has streamlined many aspects of inventory control for both manufacturers and retailers. The UPC (Universal Product Code) is used in the bar code system. EDI (Electronic Data Interchange) is the automatic transmittal of individual product-shipping and -selling information between the manufacturers and the retailers.

Each product is identified by a bar code. Goods shipped to a retailer by a manufacturer, both of whom use the EDI system bar code, are scanned when packed at the factory and an ASN (Advance Ship Notice) is electronically transmitted to the retailer. The ASN is equivalent to a packing list or invoice. When the retailer sells goods, they are also scanned at the cash register. A record of the sales or depleting inventory is electronically transferred to the manufacturer, who then learns which products need replacing.

Obviously, this system is invaluable in high-volume operations. Even if your company is not doing high volume, you may be selling to vendors who use the UPC and EDI system. Bar codes alone can easily be produced by the appropriate software. EDI software is quite costly and the formats used by the vendors vary and are constantly changing. If you have an account that requires UPC and EDI, you can use an EDI service to perform the required functions for a fee.

U.S. Customs Compliance

The apparel industry is one of eight primary-focus industries of the U.S. Customs Service, at this writing. Documentation of each step of the production and shipping process is the key to avoiding tariffs on fabric created and cut in the U.S. and then sent to the Caribbean or Mexico to be made into a finished garment. Documentation is also the key to surviving an audit.

Your internal Customs compliance program should apply to every department, from management to shipping. In creating standard invoices, purchase orders, letters of credit and supplier agreements, include language prohibiting transshipment and the mislabeling of the country of origin to avoid import quotas.

Request that your suppliers give you an affidavit on the country of origin that also states that a certificate of origin is available to Customs upon their request. Customs also wants to know how many garments are produced from a given amount of fabric; include yardage lost to flaws in your calculations. Keep your records for at least five years. Work with a licensed customs broker, as necessary.

Trade Agreements

The garment industry in the United States is coping with the economic changes created by various laws and organizations, some with these familiar acronyms:

- NAFTA—the North American Free Trade Agreement
- CBM—the Caribbean Basin Initiative
- AGOA—the Africa Growth and Opportunity Act (sub Saharan Africa)
- TDA—the Trade Development Act

Also, the U.S.'s granting of MFN—Most Favored Nation status to China (in the process of becoming a member of the WTO—World Trade Organization) by the U.S. has affected import duties. NAFTA is having a dramatic effect on garment manufacturing operations in the U.S. Many companies have all or part of their operations in Mexico. All trade agreements have complex economic, social and political ramifications for all participants in the one world in which we live.

E-commerce

E-commerce is a viable method of distributing your product at a retail level. It requires just as much business know-how as any other business, as we have learned from the recent demise of many dot.com companies. The use of the Internet for communications and distribution of information among suppliers, manufacturers, wholesalers and distributors and retailers has enhanced and simplified these operations. We should expect further improvements to communication and distribution through e-commerce.

Shipping

Packaging Materials

Should these be politically correct? How important is this to you, the customer and the planet?

- **Poly Bags**—keep the product clean. Can be used to package product in predetermined sets called prepacks.
- **Tissue Paper**—protects product.
- **String**—keeps small items of same size and fabrication together.
- **Hanger**—plastic, wooden or metal. Do not use hangers from the cleaners.

Boxes and Shipping Envelopes

- **Boxes**—new or recycled. Must be sturdy, clean and in good condition. Seal all six edges with sturdy packing tape.
- **Shipping Envelopes**—new or recycled. Tyvek or paper. Padded or unpadded. Must be sturdy, clean and in good condition. Can be used for soft goods. Seal flap with tape.
- **Paperwork**—use your original order for your checkoff sheet when packing. Include a packing slip (no prices indicated) or invoice (prices indicated) inside the box or padded shipping envelope or in a plastic pocket attached to the outside of the box or envelope. Send a copy of the invoice to the appropriate sales rep the same day that the order ships.
- **Insurance**—most shippers (UPS, RPS, etc.) provide free insurance on the first $100 of declared value of each package. It is a good idea to insure the package for its full value. Usually the cost is included in the shipping charges and paid by the retailer. Sometimes you pay the insurance.

Shipping to Large Chains, Department Stores and Conglomerates

These are usually big orders and it feels like a feather in your cap to count them among your accounts. Along with those positive aspects come a few harsh realities:

- Each store or chain has a book of rules that contains very exacting instructions on how the goods are to be packaged, labeled and shipped. (Shipping to these large accounts is usually to their distribution centers from which goods are then sent to the individual stores.)

- Any deviation by you will result in *CHARGE BACKS*: the store will deduct varying amounts of money from your payment for incorrectly following procedures.

- PAY ATTENTION TO AND FOLLOW ALL THEIR RULES.

When to Ship Your Orders

Orders should always be shipped to arrive by or on the requested delivery date, regardless of whether you ship "as ready," daily or weekly. You can ship within the delivery-date window as the orders are packed and ready, or you can ship once a week. Your contract with UPS or RPS will include a daily pickup stop by the driver whether or not you have packages going out on any given day.

Incomplete Orders

These can occur because of fabric or production delays or accidental shortages. Ship as much of the order as you can and indicate on the invoice what is back-ordered and when you expect to ship it. If the partial shipment is part of a set of two—a coordinated top and bottom, for example—contact your customers about the split shipment so that they are aware of the situation. They may request that you withhold the entire shipment until the order is complete or they may want you to ship the partially complete order.

When you know in advance that some items will ship late, either send a postcard notice or phone your accounts and let them know of the delay ahead of time. If there is a problem, they will let you know. In the meantime, you are on top of the situation—a better place to be than behind the eight ball.

An industry-specific or basic data-based software program allows you to input orders by customer, develop tallies and make lists of what to produce. This program will create packing lists, invoices, statements and past-due notices and generate dollar totals of orders shipped and accounts receivable ledgers. A definitely advantageous tool.

Reorders

Can you ship them from available inventory? If not, at what point do you produce them and how much do you actually produce? Just the amount of the reorders or extra to cover future reorders? There is no blanket rule. Use your best guesstimating abilities.

Excess Inventory

How do you move these goods on out and still make some profit?

*   Reduce the price.
*   Generate sales by sending out postcards or fliers to your mailing lists or by posting notices online at auction sites.
*   Make phone calls to accounts that have bought these items in the past and other good accounts to which you sell.
*   Sell to stores that deal in closeouts.

If all else fails, you can donate excess goods and receive either a personal deduction, if you are not incorporated, or a corporate deduction if you are incorporated.

Collecting Your Money

Nothing beats getting money in the mail. But sometimes it can be hard work and take a long time to actually get paid for goods that you have shipped to stores. The use of factors (see the Glossary) and credit cards to get payment from your accounts can greatly increase the amount of money you receive on time from your billable accounts. And remember that the check in the mail that finally arrives may bounce when you deposit it! Not fun. (Photocopy both sides of the check and redeposit it immediately. This is the first step in dealing with bad checks. Next, you will involve a local sheriff or process server. You can obtain specifics on how to proceed from the local law enforcement agency *where the bad check was written.*)

Try to remember that it is just money. Any problems are the drivel and frustration and reality of doing business and not a reflection on the worth of you or your product. Yes, you have paid for the materials, labor and shipping. Yes, you have paid for the trade shows and all your other selling tools. Yes, your overhead costs do not go on hold until the money arrives. But, try not to become too stressed over the money, because your stress will not change the realities.

You bill Net 30 from the day you ship; stores pay Net 30 from the day they receive the goods. Deal with this gap area as follows: Send your statement on your Net 30 date. Start *your* Friendly Phone Calls a few days after their Net 30 date. In reality, stores may be paying you at Net 60, 90 or even 120 days.

Cash-Flow ("Out" Before "In") Chart

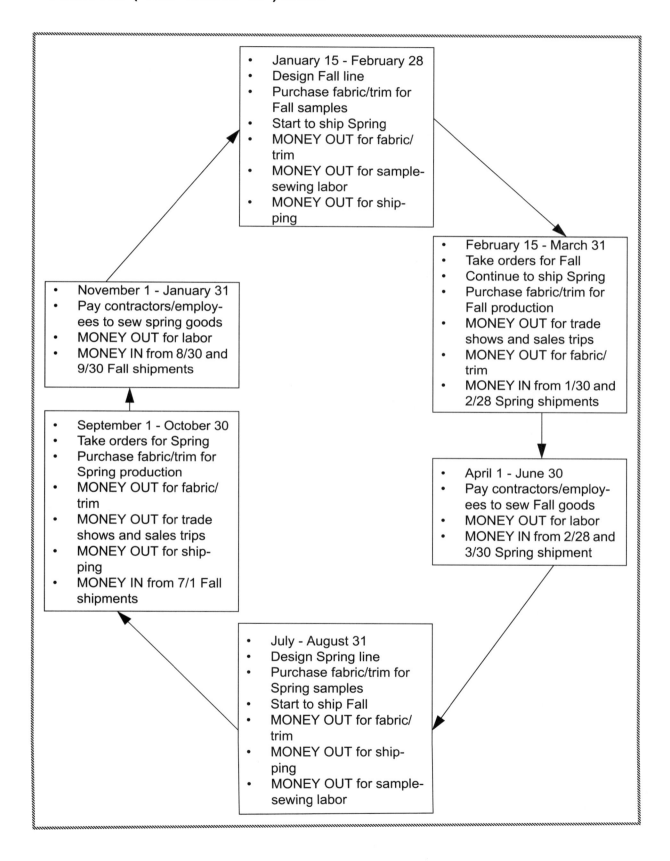

- January 15 - February 28
- Design Fall line
- Purchase fabric/trim for Fall samples
- Start to ship Spring
- MONEY OUT for fabric/trim
- MONEY OUT for sample-sewing labor
- MONEY OUT for shipping

- February 15 - March 31
- Take orders for Fall
- Continue to ship Spring
- Purchase fabric/trim for Fall production
- MONEY OUT for trade shows and sales trips
- MONEY OUT for fabric/trim
- MONEY IN from 1/30 and 2/28 Spring shipments

- November 1 - January 31
- Pay contractors/employees to sew spring goods
- MONEY OUT for labor
- MONEY IN from 8/30 and 9/30 Fall shipments

- April 1 - June 30
- Pay contractors/employees to sew Fall goods
- MONEY OUT for labor
- MONEY IN from 2/28 and 3/30 Spring shipment

- September 1 - October 30
- Take orders for Spring
- Purchase fabric/trim for Spring production
- MONEY OUT for fabric/trim
- MONEY OUT for trade shows and sales trips
- MONEY OUT for shipping
- MONEY IN from 7/1 Fall shipments

- July - August 31
- Design Spring line
- Purchase fabric/trim for Spring samples
- Start to ship Fall
- MONEY OUT for fabric/trim
- MONEY OUT for shipping
- MONEY OUT for sample-sewing labor

The above cash-flow chart is true for every selling season throughout the year, although it focuses on the two traditional major selling seasons. Plan for a six- to nine-month turn around on your investment.

The following is an outline of what you can do to collect your unpaid invoices. It can be a complex and expensive proposition to put an account in collection. You will receive only a percentage of the amount due and will have to pay legal fees on top of that. If you find yourself in this situation regularly you should join a credit rating service and use the information it provides to decide who you will produce for and ship to. The amount of money you will save will be worth every penny it will cost to belong to the service.

"I'm just waiting for those checks 'in the mail'."

Orderly Steps to Collect Your Money

- Include a copy of the invoice with the order.
- Mail the original invoice the day the order ships.
- Mail a statement 30 days after the date of the original invoice, which includes 1.5 percent interest per month on outstanding charges.
- Make "friendly" phone calls: "How is the product doing?"   "When can I expect my money?"
- Mail a statement at 45 days that includes interest on the balance due.
- Make more phone calls.
- Send a statement at 60 days that includes interest on the balance due.
- Make more phone calls.
- Send a statement at 90 days that includes interest on the balance due.

- Notify the account that nonpayment of outstanding charges will result in the account being sent for collection.
- Hire a collection agency.

Additional Ways to Collect Your Money and Counter Your Losses

- Involve the sales rep who wrote the order in collecting your money. Remember that the sales rep does not get paid until you do.
- Stop producing for, and shipping additional orders to, that account.
- Physically remove your remaining merchandise from the store.

FINAL ANALYSIS

Congratulations! You have made it through your first run of design-based manufacturing. Undoubtedly, you have learned many new things, including many shortcuts and have been confounded by many others. On your next go-around you will be able to look ahead to plan your actions more effectively. You will be operating from a position of strength and knowledge. As you continue gaining experience, you will continue improving your design-based manufacturing skills.

We hope that we have guided and educated you. We welcome your comments and feedback so that this book can be the best we can offer.

Keep your business "feet" on the ground and your creative "head" in the clouds.

Rice Crispies:
The Entrepreneurial Explosion

GLOSSARY

ACCOUNTS PAYABLE—All your current accounts (suppliers) to whom you owe money.

ACCOUNTS RECEIVABLE—All your current accounts (stores, catalogs) who owe you money.

BODIES—The basic shapes or silhouettes of the garments or accessories that you design and manufacture.

BOOTH—The space you rent at a trade show in which to display and sell your products.

BREAK-EVEN POINT—The point at which annual sales cover related costs and expenses—without profit and without loss. The point at which total income equals total expenditure: The income after this point is profit.

BUNDLING—The act of putting cut pieces together by size and/or color; all pieces in a bundle are sewn and then the bundle proceeds to its next step in the assembling of the garment. For example, all the right sleeves of Style 3003 Blue, Size 10, are bundled together and sewn. The bundle of completed sleeves then proceeds to the next station where the sleeves are attached to the bodies of the Size 10 blue blouses, another bundle.   A few workers will operate a variety of sewing machines as needed.

BUTTONHOLE/BUTTON-SEW SERVICES—Contractors who sew buttonholes and buttons at predetermined prices using specialized sewing machines.

BUYERS—People employed by or representing stores, catalogs or Internet sales venues whose job is to purchase goods to be sold in stores, in catalogs or online.

CAD—Computer Assisted Design. Software used in designing, pattern making and grading.

CANCEL DATE—The date on which an order cancels if it has not yet been delivered or shipped.

CARE LABELS or TAGS—The labels and tags required by the Federal Trade Commission's Permanent Care Labeling Regulation, 1972 (amended 1984). The FTC requires that manufacturers or importers of textile wearing apparel and certain piece goods provide a permanent attached and legible label or tag that contains regular care instructions about washing, drying, ironing, bleaching and dry cleaning and any information about warnings. As of July 1997, approved care symbols can be used in place of written instructions on permanent labels. The regulation specifies the location of the label by garment type—basically where it is most visible to the consumer. Check the FTC pamphlet "Writing a Care Label" for specifics.

CMT (Cut, Make, Trim)—An acronym referring to the steps in producing a finished garment from yardage. The pattern pieces of the garment, accessory or sewn product are cut. The garment, accessory or sewn product is made. The item is trimmed with buttons, ribbon, etc., and tagged. The term is often used by the contractor or person producing your garments to quote you a cost for work to be done.

COLD CALLS—Sales calls by phone or in person, without prior appointments. These are neither a good sales method nor the most comfortable situation. But sometimes they are quite necessary to get your product out there.

COLLECTION—Your product line(s) for a given selling season.

COLLECTION AGENCIES—Companies that collect money on past-due accounts; their fee is usually one-third of the amount owed. Sometimes, lawyers fees are added.

COMMISSION—Money paid to a sales rep for selling your product or service—usually a percentage of the wholesale cost. Normally, the commission rate for apparel is 10 percent and for accessories 15 to 20 percent.

COMPANY NAME—The name by which a business is known. It is usually the same as the fictitious business name, or dba (Doing Business As).

CONTRACTOR—A person or company that performs work on a large scale at a predetermined price according to a contractual agreement.

CONVERTER—A person or company that oversees and/or performs the change of plain fabrics and greige goods into finished goods through any processes applied or done to the fabric, such as printing, waterproofing, stonewashing or dyeing.

COPYRIGHT—The exclusive right to publish, produce or sell the rights to original works of art (literary, dramatic, musical or artistic) fixed in a tangible medium of expression. Copyright is granted by law for a specified period of time. To be copyrightable, a work must contain a certain minimum amount of original expression. Copyright does not protect ideas, methods, systems or principles, nor layout, coloring and lettering.

CPFR (Collaborative Planning Forecasting and Replenishment)—A software process that interfaces all entities in a supply chain, within and without a company.

CREDIT-RATING SERVICES—Companies that collect and supply credit information on individuals and businesses.

CUTTERS—Contractors who cut yardage into pattern pieces at predetermined prices by using scissors, rotary cutters (electric and hand), fabric saws or laser cutters.

DBA—See FICTITIOUS BUSINESS NAME.

DELIVERY DATES—The date on which, or window of dates during which, a store requests delivery of its order. For example, an August 1 delivery date means that the store wishes to take delivery on August 1. "August 1 through August 15" means that the store wishes to take delivery sometime during that two-week period. "August 1, cancel August 15" means that the store will take delivery between August 1 and August 15; and if they have not received the goods by August 15 the order is automatically canceled.

DESIGNERS— People who create textile, apparel and/or sewn product designs.

DESIGN SPEC SHEET—A worksheet that shows all the specifications for each item to be produced (one Design Spec Sheet per item). It should also include fabric swatches and a sketch of the item being manufactured.

DIRECT SALES—Selling directly to the consumer with no middleman (sales rep, store, catalog). Ensures direct communication between the seller (and maker) of the product and the end consumer.

DISTRIBUTOR—This middle person distributes goods between the wholesaler and/or the garment manufacturer and/or the retail store. (Many possibilities.)

DYE HOUSE—The plant where fabric or piece goods are dyed.

EAS (Electronic Article Surveillance)—Anti-theft electronic codes embedded in sewn or hang tags and labels and in design elements of garments and read by scanners at exits of retail establishments.

E-BUSINESS and E-COMMERCE—Business conducted on or through the Internet.

EDI (Electronic Data Interchange)—The automatic transmittal of individual-product shipping and selling information between manufacturers and retailers.

EMBROIDERERS—Contractors who embroider apparel or sewn products at predetermined prices, usually using computer-driven embroidering sewing machines.

FABRIC SHOWS—Trade shows at which fabric and trim are sold at wholesale prices to manufacturers and fabric stores.

FABRICATIONS—The specific fabrics used to make a particular garment, accessory or sewn product, which may vary by type, color, pattern or weight.

FABRICS—The cloth materials made of fibers or yarns out of which garments, accessories or other sewn products are produced.

FACTORS—Commercial banks or finance companies specializing in financial services to producers and dealers. They provide a credit reference for manufacturers to their suppliers and pay the suppliers. They check the credit rating of a manufacturer's accounts and collect payments to manufacturers. They can advance money to manufacturers on the basis of orders in-house, orders in production and accounts receivable. Factors do business with companies that gross a minimum of $2 million to $3 million.

FIBER-CONTENT LABELS—Labels required by the Textile Fiber Products Identification Act, 1960 (amended 1986). The following information, in English, is required on the label or tag of most textile items. The tag can be placed at the point of entry to the garment or in a side seam. The percentages of all fibers in each textile are listed in order of predominance by weight.The full name of the manufacturer or the company's registered number (RN#). The name of the country where the product was processed or manufactured. The country of origin is identified as the country where the item is assembled.

FICTITIOUS BUSINESS NAME/DBA (Doing Business As)—A business name—usually a company name—registered in the county and state in which the company does business. A fictitious business name cannot include the full surname of the person doing business. All individuals, partnerships or other associations that regularly transact business for profit doing business under a fictitious business name must file a fictitious business name statement. The holder of the fictitious business name has the exclusive use of that name in the state in which it is registered, usually, a five-year renewable periods; that time period may vary in different states. In order to open a business checking account and often to obtain a local business license or resale tax license a business must file a fictitious name statement.

FIRST COST—The basic combined cost of the materials and labor necessary to produce one item; may be referred to as the **cost to manufacture one item**.

FIRST PATTERN—The initial pattern of an item made after the prototype and from which samples are made. It may require adjustments or reworking to ensure proper fit and style for production.

FIXED COSTS—Overhead or operating costs not directly related to the production of a specific product or service, such as the cost of rent, phone, FedEx, insurance premiums, professional fees, employee expenses, and office supplies.

FIXTURES—Items used for display purposes in showrooms, trade show booths and retail stores.

FREIGHT CHARGES—The fees charged for shipping goods.

GARMENT MANUFACTURERS' LICENSE AND REGISTRATION—Required by law and strictly enforced in some states to ensure adherence to labor laws. Usually, the completion of a complicated form, the taking of a test based on labor law, and the payment of a fee are the requirements for a license and registration.

GRADERS—Individuals who create pattern pieces in a full size range from a basic pattern. This can be done manually or with CAD programs.

GREIGE or GRAY GOODS—Fabrics which have not been bleached, processed or converted in any manner.

HANGTAGS—Tags attached to garments which provide product identification and product information: Care tags and fiber content tags, as well as company ID/logo tags that give style, size and color information are examples of hangtags.

HORIZONTAL BUSINESS GROUPS—A level of business, across the board, performing the same function. For example, the design departments of many companies are connected, often by software, in a business venture creating a horizontal structure. Or the horizontal level of all designers is the focus of a sales operation by a software company.

HOUSE ACCOUNT—An account initiated and maintained by the manufacturer; no fee is paid to any sales rep.

IMAGE—A public view of one's company and products, often indicative of its nature or quality; the impression the company wishes to create and convey.

IN-HOUSE PRODUCTION—The cutting and sewing or manufacturing of goods within the confines of the company, not farmed out to contractors.

IN-LINE (ASSEMBLY-LINE) PRODUCTION—A type of production in which each piece of each garment is sewn individually and then passed on to the next person in the line, who performs the next function. Generally, there is one person working at each machine or station. This type is common throughout the world, with the exception of the U.S.

INVOICE—An itemized bill that lists the merchandise costs, shipping and C.O.D. charges and insurance charges. It is included with the shipment inside the box or in a plastic pocket on the outside of the box and/or mailed to the customer.

JOBBER—A person or company that buys end or odd lots of fabrics from mills, converters, wholesalers and distributors or from garment, accessory and sewn product manufacturers at reduced rates and resells them at reduced rates. Small quantities can be purchased from them, but usually there is no continuity in the availability of a fabric, design or color. Some jobbers do carry continuous stock of some solids and basics.

KEYSTONING—The doubling of costs to determine a sales price: manufacturers set a price that is double their costs when selling to retailers, and retailers double their costs when pricing goods to sell to consumers.

KNITS—Fabrics constructed by joining loops of yarn, either by hand with knitting needles or by machine. T-shirts and sweaters are made of knits.

LINE SHEET—A sheet (or sheets) of detailed information and sketches/photos of a product line that is used as a selling tool and is updated each season. See PRODUCT LINE.

LOGO—A graphic or visual identifier of a business. A single symbol, which may include both words and symbols, that represents the name of a company or an advertiser's trademark.

MANUFACTURER—A company/person that designs products, controls all or parts of production and sells directly to retailers.

MARKER—1) Pattern pieces are laid out on a roll of marker paper, which has a one-inch grid printed on it; the paper comes in yardage widths up to 90 inches. The completed marker is then laid out on the full width and length of the fabric to be cut. It is held in place with staples, pushpins, weights or tape. 2) A master cutting plan for the pattern pieces of a specific style.

MARKET DAYS OR WEEKS—Selling periods that occur regularly at specific times throughout the year in trade-mart buildings in various cities throughout the country.

MARKET FEES—Fees paid to a merchandise-mart building association for rental of temporary space during market days/weeks.

MARKUP—An amount added to the cost of goods to create profit; it includes the overhead and profit margin of both manufacturer and retailer. It is usually a predetermined percentage. First cost plus markup equals wholesale price. Wholesale cost plus markup equals retail price.

MART—A building of selling showrooms usually located in a major city. Some marts are dedicated to a specific type of merchandise—clothing, home decor, jewelry, etc.

MILL—A factory or plant where fabric is knit or woven.

MINIMUM ORDER—The least dollar value or number of items required to place an order; for example, "Minimum Order $100." This information should appear on the line sheet.

MODULAR MANUFACTURING—A type of manufacturing in which the team members are cross-trained to perform various functions in producing a finished product; this approach develops problem-solving skills. Generally, such workers reduce the throughput time of a finished product, establish in-line quality control and take care of equipment. Pay is based on achieving goals, not on a piece or task rate.

ORDER FORM—The form used by a salesperson to write an order from a customer. The information from this form is then used for production, shipping and billing purposes.

OUTSOURCING—Obtaining and using goods or services from outside the company.

OVERHEAD—Costs not directly related to the production of a specific product or service. See FIXED COSTS.

PACKAGING—The materials used for shipping goods; the way the goods are available for sale, e.g., in boxes of one dozen per size.

PACKING LIST—A form that itemizes the items included in a shipment and indicates any items on back order or sold out. The packing list is placed either inside the shipping box or inside a plastic pocket on the outside of the shipping box.

PATENT—A government document granting an inventor or designer of a specific process, method or system for a stated period of time; the exclusive right to make, use and sell an invention or design. *Design* patents for construction applications are used in the garment and textile design industries. These patents do not cover the textile or garment designs themselves; they are copyrightable.

PATTERN GRADERS—See GRADERS.

PATTERNMAKERS—People who make patterns used in the development and manufacture of apparel and sewn products.

PIECE—A finished individual garment or accessory such as a shirt or a pair of pants.

PIECE GOODS—Yard goods; textiles made in standard widths and usually sold by the yard. Also, manufactured goods that are sold by the piece.

POLY BAGS—Plastic bags used for packaging a product individually or in predetermined sets or prepacks.

POSITIONING STATEMENT—A tight, seven- to ten-word description of the designer's or manufacture's core concept or intention.

PREPACKS—Goods that are sold in a predetermined assortment of sizes or colors.

PRICE POINT—The actual wholesale price for which a product is sold.

PRODUCT LINE—The cohesive group of items that a company produces for sale at wholesale.

PRODUCTION PATTERNS—The final versions of a pattern, in the full size range offered, that are used to make a marker (see MARKER) to cut the pieces used in production sewing.

PRODUCTION SEWERS—People who operate production- or power-sewing machines. These machines operate approximately three times faster than home sewing machines and have very specialized functions.

PRODUCTS—The items that an individual or a company produces for sale at a wholesale or retail level.

PROFIT—The sum remaining after all the direct and indirect costs of producing and marketing goods have been subtracted from the sales income.

PROTOTYPE—The first creation of the item being designed. It may come before a pattern is made. It can be a mock-up of what the item should look like or it can be the first sample that is sewn together.

PULLING and PACKING—The process of retrieving and boxing goods to fill each specific order.

QUALITY CONTROL/QUALITY ASSURANCE—The process of checking every step of production, from cutting through labeling and packaging, to find flawed goods or procedures—flawed fabric, irregularly cut pieces, improperly sewn goods, flawed or missing trim, improper tagging and packaging. You want to ship first-quality goods that will not be returned because of poor quality. To accept and replace returned goods will cost you two to three times the cost of producing and shipping your original goods.

REORDERS—Repeat orders of goods by a store or catalog.

REPEAT BODIES—Silhouettes or body styles presented in various fabrications and with various modifications, such as adding pleats or pockets, shortening or lengthening or changing a collar shape.

RESALE LICENSE/SALES TAX LICENSE—A license issued by states charging sales tax. The sales tax is collected at the point of final sale to the consumer. Companies and individuals who buy goods, in the process of creating the final product sold to the consumer, obtain a license from the state; this exempts them from paying tax on goods or components of goods which will ultimately be resold and on which sales tax will be collected. To obtain this license it is usually necessary to have a Fictitious Business Name/DBA and to be able to show proof that your business qualifies for such a license. If a person obtains a license and does not resell goods that he has purchased tax-exempt, his resale license will be pulled in short order.

RETAIL—The direct sale of goods to consumers; the point at which the sales tax is collected.

RETAIL COST OR PRICE—The cost paid by the ultimate consumer at a retail outlet.

RISER—A display fixture that creates additional levels of display space on tabletops. Used at trade shows and in showrooms.

ROAD REPS—Salespeople who travel to stores to do their selling rather than selling from a showroom.

ROAD TRIPS—Trips taken for selling purposes by traveling sales reps, road reps, or other persons selling a line.

RPS—Roadway Package Service, a firm that picks up and delivers packages from business to business only, throughout the world. Manufacturers may contract with RPS to pick up packages and deliver them to their accounts.

SALES SAMPLES—The items produced for use by the people who sell a product: the designer/manufacturer or the sales reps.

SALES TERMS—The conditions of a sale stating how payment will be made for the order. *See "Credit Terminology" on page 75.*

SAMPLE MAKERS—People who sew the prototypes and the first, selling and production samples.

SCM—Supply Chain Management, a type of software dedicated to connecting the suppliers and the users of the supply chain in a company: designers, vendors and contractors, for example.

SCREEN PRINTER—A plant where a design is printed on fabric or piece goods (T-shirts, for instance).

SELLING SEASONS—*Traditionally*: Spring, Summer, Fall and Winter/Holiday/Resort seasons. Spring sells in September/October; deliveries are 1/30-3/31. Summer sells in January; deliveries are 4/15-5/31. Fall sells in March; deliveries are 6/30-9/30. Winter/Holiday/Resort sells in June and August; deliveries are 10/1-12/15. (*See "Selling Seasons and Marketing Calendar" on page 59.*)

SHIPPING AND DISTRIBUTION—The process of delivering goods from the manufacturer to the buyers.

SHOWROOM—A room used by a sales rep to display goods for sale at a mart building or other business structure. Often, smaller companies have showrooms at their factories.

SHOWROOM FEE—The cost of renting space in a sales rep's showroom. In major cities, it is often necessary to pay a rep showroom fees, in addition to a commission.

SILHOUETTES—See BODIES; STYLE.

SKU—Stock Keeping Unit: A computerized number assigned to each size and color fabrication of an item, used for tracking and ordering purposes.

SLOGAN—Word or phrase used to express a characteristic position, stand or goal.

SNAP SETTERS—People who set snaps at predetermined prices using specialized machinery.

SPECS—Specifications or enumerations of the particulars of fabric and trim, production, and so on.

SPLIT COMMISSION—A sales commission shared by two or more reps or by a house account and a sales rep. This split happens when territories overlap or when more than one person is involved in a sale, for any reason.

STATEMENT—A bill for all outstanding charges a customer owes, including finance charges for late payment; generally mailed every thirty days, as needed.

START DATE—The first date on which an order can be delivered or shipped.

STYLE—A particular shape, silhouette or look of a garment or other item.

STYLE NAME—The name assigned to each particular style, such as Granny Skirt or Slinky Top. This information should appear on sample tags, line sheets and hangtags.

STYLE NUMBER—A number assigned to each particular style. This number should appear on sample tags, line sheets and hangtags.

SUBCONTRACTOR—A person or company that contracts to perform part or all of another's contract.

SWATCHCARD—A paper card to which are attached small pieces (1" x 2" +/-) of all the fabrications (color, print or fabric types) in which a particular style or set of styles is available.

TEXTILE WHOLESALER—Either the textile manufacturer or another company that sells the textile manufacturer's product. Usually, there are two wholesale divisions. One sells to garment, accessory and sewn product manufacturers and requires large minimum orders of thousands of yards; the other sells to retail fabric stores, at slightly higher wholesale prices than those charged to the manufacturers, but in the small quantities that are needed by a start-up or small manufacturer.

TRADE SHOW—A themed selling venue in a major market area: for example, a sporting goods show at the Los Angeles Coliseum or a kids' clothing and accessory show in New York City at the Javits Center.

TRADEMARK—A word, phrase, symbol or design, or a combination of those, which identifies and distinguishes the source of the goods or services of one party from those of others; usually registered and protected by law. In addition to accepting protection of the identity of a product or service, a designer/manufacturer must diligently go after anyone infringing on his trademark: the trademark assures the public of an identifiable product or service. Receiving the trademark also includes receiving a mandate to protect the public.

TRIMS—Ribbon, lace, zippers, buttons, bows and other items, both functional and decorative, used in finishing a garment or sewn product.

UNITS—Pieces, as in: "How many units of this style are we producing?"

UPS—United Parcel Service, a firm that picks up and delivers packages throughout the world. A manufacturer may contract with UPS to pick up packages and deliver them to her accounts.

URL—Uniform Resource Locator, or an address on the World Wide Web.

VARIABLE COSTS—Expenses that are directly proportional to the amount of net sales (e.g., selling commissions, net shipping expenses).

VERTICAL STRUCTURE—The entire structure of a business from top to bottom; an organizational tool or software used to address issues within the structure.

WHOLESALE—Indirect selling to consumers via retail stores or catalogs; no sales tax is collected.

WHOLESALE COST—The *first cost* plus *markup*. Also, the cost of goods paid by retailers.

WHOLESALER—Either the manufacturer or another company that sells the manufacturer's product to retailers.

WOVEN—Fabrics that are constructed by weaving or interlacing threads, yarns or strips of fibrous material. Denim used for jeans and sheeting used for bed sheets are examples of woven fabrics.

APPENDIX A: BIBLIOGRAPHY

Books

Anatomy of a Business Plan, Linda Pinson and Jerry Jinnett. Dearborn, 1995.

The Apparel Design and Production Hand Book, Fashiondex, Inc., 1998.

Apparel Manufacturing: Sewn Product Analysis, Ruth E. Glock and Grace Kunz. Prentice Hall, 1999.

Apparel Product Design, Maurice J. Johnson and Evelyn Moore. Prentice Hall, 2001.

Best Dressed, Suzy Gershman. Three Rivers Press, 2000.

The Business of Fashion, Leslie Davis Burns and Nancy O. Bryant. Fairchild Publications, 1997.

CAD for Fashion Design, Renee Weiss Chase. Prentice Hall, 1997.

Crafting as a Business, Wendy W. Rosen. The Rosen Group Inc., 1994.

The Craft's Business Answer Book & Resource Guide: Answers to Hundreds of Troublesome Questions about Starting, Marketing and Managing a Homebased Business, Barbara Brabec. M. Evans & Company, 1998.

The Eleven Commandments of Wildly Successful Women, Pamela Boucher Gilbeard and Audrey Tayse Hayners. Hungry Minds, Inc., 1998.

The End of Fashion: How Marketing Changed the Clothing Business Forever, Teri Agins. Harper Collins, 2000.

The Entrepreneur's Guide to Sewn Product Manufacturing, Kathleen Fasanella. Apparel Technical Services Inc., 1998.

Fabric Reference and *Fabric Glossary* (a companion swatch book), Mary Humphries. Prentice Hall, 2000.

Fabric Reference Series: All About Silk (1992), *All About Wool* (1996), *All About Cotton* (1998), Julie Parker. Rain City Publishing.

Fabric Savvy: The Essential Guide for Every Sewer, Sandra Betzina. Taunton Press, 1999.

Fabric Science, 7th ed., Joseph Pizzuto. Fairchild, 1999.

Fairchild's Dictionary of Textiles, Phyllis G. Tortora and Robert S. Merkel, eds. Fairchild Publications, 1996.

Fashion for Profit: From Design Concept to Apparel Manufacturing: A Professional's Complete Guide, Frances Harder. Frances Harder, 2000.

Homemade Money, Barbara Brabec. Betterway Books, 1994.

How to Make Your Design Business Profitable, Joyce M. Stewart. Northlight Books, 1992.

How to Say It for Women: Communicating with Confidence and Power Using the Language of Success, Phyllis Mindell. Prentice Hall, 2001.

How to Start Making Money with Your Sewing, Karen L. Maslowski. Betterway Books, 1998.

Jump Start Your Brain, Doug Hall and David Wecker (contributor). Warner Books, 1996.

Inside the Fashion Business, 6th ed., Jeanette Jarrow and Kitty Dickerson. Merrill Education, 1997.

Legal Guide for Visual Artists, 3rd ed., Tad Crawford. Allsworth Press, 1995.

Make a Name for Yourself: Eight Steps Every Woman Needs to Create a Personal Brand Strategy for Success, Robin Fisher Roffer. Broadway Books, 2000.

Minding Her Own Business: The Self-Employed Woman's Guide to Taxes and Recordkeeping, Jan Zobel. East Hill Press, 1997.

On Your Own: A Woman's Guide to Building a Business, Laurie Zuckerman. Upstart Publishing, 1990.

Sew to Success!, Kathleen Spike. Palmer/Pletsch, 1991.

Sew Up a Storm: All the Way to the Bank, Karen L. Maslowski. Sew Storm Publishing, 1995.

Sewing for the Apparel Industry, Claire Shaeffer. Prentice Hall, 2001.

Small-Time Operator, Bernard B. Kamoroff. Bell Springs Publishing, 1997.

Start and Run a Profitable Catering Business, Self Counsel Press Inc.,1994.

Start Your Own Gift Basket Business, Business Concepts. Pfeiffer and Company, 1994.

A Stitch in Time: Lean Retailing and the Transformation of Manufacturing: Lessons from the Apparel and Textile Industries, Frederick H. Abernathy, John T. Dunlop, Janice Hammond, David Weil. Oxford University Press, 1999.

Techno Fabrics, Sarah Braddock and Marie O'Mahony. Thames and Hudson,1998.

The Upstart Guide to Owning and Managing a Bar and Tavern, Dearborn Publishing, 1995.

The World of Fashion, 2nd ed., Jay Diamond and Ellen Diamond. Fairchild Publications, 1997.

You Can Make Money from Your Arts and Crafts: The Arts and Crafts Marketing Book, Steve and Cindy Long. Mark Publishing, 1988.

Periodicals

Apparel News Group, Subscription Service Department, 107 W. Van Buren, Ste. 204, Chicago, IL 60605; 312-583-1211; www.apparelnews.net. Publishers, currently, of *California Apparel News* and *Waterwear*, with seasonal inserts for *Market Week Magazine, New York Apparel News, Dallas Apparel News, Apparel News South, Chicago Apparel News, The Apparel News* (National), *Bridal Apparel News, Southwest Images, Stylist* and *Man* (Men's Apparel News). These weekly and quarterly publications cover fashion industry news with a focus on regional and topical companies and markets.

Bobbin The Apparel Industry Magazine, PO Box 1986 1500 Hampton St., Ste. 150 Columbia, SC 29202; 800-845-8820, 803-771-7500; FAX 803-799-1461. Published monthly with information on all sewn products industries.

Fairchild Publications, 7 W. 34th St., New York, NY 10001; 800-289-0273; www. fairchildpub.com. Publishers of books and the following periodicals: *Women's Wear Daily*—covers national and international news in the fashion industry, *DNR* (Daily News Record)—covers national and international news in menswear and textile industries; *Children's Business*—published monthly for retailers of children's products; *Sportstyle*—sportswear and sports equipment published 18 times a year, *Footwear News*—published Mondays covering the national and international shoe industry; *W*—a glossy fashion industry gossip magazine published monthly; *HFN* (Home Furnishing News)—a weekly about furniture, housewares, textiles, consumer electronics and computers; *JANE*—a lifestyle magazine for women 18-34; and *Details*—a lifestyle magazine for men 25-34.

Power Sewing, Sandra Betzina's weekly syndicated column in newspapers throughout the country.

SewNews, PJS Publications, Inc. Monthly. Newsstand and subscription.

Threads, Taunton Press. Bimonthly. Newsstand and subscription.

112

APPENDIX B: SOURCES

Year-Round Fabric and Industry Information

NEW WEBSITES ARE CONSTANTLY APPEARING WITH INFORMATION ABOUT TEXTILES AND OTHER ASPECTS OF THE GARMENT MANUFACTURING BUSINESS.

AAFA (AMERICAN APPAREL AND FOOTWEAR ASSOCIATION) 1601 N. Kent St., Ste. 1200, Arlington, VA 22209; 800-520-2262; www.americanapparel.org. Membership consists of major manufacturers of apparel and footwear. (Merger of AAMA, FIA and TFA.)

AAPN (AMERICAN APPAREL PRODUCERS NETWORK) Box 720693, Atlanta, GA 30358; 404-843-3171; www.usawear.org. Members are producers and contractors of quality authentic American apparel.

AMERICAN TEXTILE MANUFACTURERS INSTITUTE 1130 Connecticut Ave. N.W., Ste. 1200, Washington, DC 20036-3954; 202-862-0500; www.atmi.org. News and information, from members, about the U.S. textile industry.

APPAREL EXCHANGE 814 E. Livingston Court, Marietta, GA 30067; 888-455-2940; www.fabric.com. Fabric clearinghouse: who has what fabric to sell; usually odd lots.

CALIFORNIA APPAREL NEWS 110 E. 9th St., Ste. A-777, Los Angeles, CA 90079-1777; 213-627-3737; www.apparelnews.net.

CALIFORNIA FASHION ASSOCIATION 515 S. Flower St. 32nd Floor, Los Angeles, CA 90071; 213-688-6288; www.californiafashion.org. California fashion industry forum consisting of manufacturers, suppliers, allied associations and professional support people.

COTTON, INC. 488 Madison Ave. New York, NY 10022; 212-413-8300; www.cottoninc.com. Providers of information about cotton, its qualities, specific sources, color forecasts and hot links to other sites.

ETEXX 306 W. 38th St., Ste. 508, New York, NY 10018; 646-473-0880; www.etexx.com. Textile and technology news trends and sourcing.

FABRIC MARKETING RESEARCH 16 Catalpa Lane, Valley Stream, NY 11581; 212-686-2345 www.fabricmarketing.com. Daily updates of information for apparel, textile and soft-goods industries. Large accessible database for apparel and fabric.

FAIRCHILD PUBLICATIONS 7 W. 34th St., New York, NY 10001; 800-289-0273; www.fairchildpub.com. Publishers of books and the following periodicals: *Women's Wear Daily*—covers national and international news in the fashion industry, *DNR* (Daily News Record)—covers national and international news in menswear and textile industries; *Children's Business*—published monthly for retailers of children's products; *Sportstyle*—sportswear and sports equipment published 18 times a year, *Footwear News*—published Mondays covering the national and international shoe industry; *W*—a glossy fashion industry gossip magazine published monthly; *HFN* (Home Furnishing News)—a weekly about furniture, housewares, textiles, consumer electronics and computers; *JANE*—a lifestyle magazine for women 18-34; and *Details*—a lifestyle magazine for men 25-34.

FASHIONDEX 153 W. 27th St., Ste. 700, New York, NY 10001; 212-647-0051; Fax 212-691-5873; www.fashiondex.com. Publisher and distributor of apparel industry information. Check online for specifics.

FIBERWORLD www.fiberworld.com. An online fiber classroom with easy-to-follow information.

GO TEXAN 1720 Regal Row, Ste. 118; Dallas, TX 75235; 214-951-9655; www.agr.state.tx.us. Promoters of Texas-grown or -shorn natural fibers; fabric must be 60 percent cotton, wool or mohair.

INDUSTRIAL FABRICS ASSOCIATION INTERNATIONAL 1801 W. County Rd. B, Roseville, MN 55113; 800-225-4324; www.ifai.com. Trade association for fabric manufacturers, suppliers and distributors of industrial fabrics and end-product manufacturers using industrial fabrics—basically anything outside the home: awnings, marine, aviation.

MASTERS OF LINEN 200 Lexington Ave., Ste. 225, New York, NY 10016; 212-734-3640 and 210-725-0483. They represent linen mills and supply information about and sources of linen yardage.

NADEIM (THE NATIONAL ASSOCIATION OF DESIGNER ENTREPRENEURS AND INDEPEN-DENT MANUFACTURERS) PO Box 98, Fort Stanton, NM 88323-0098; 505-354-3344; pattrn-makr@zianet.com. Members are design entrepreneurs.

NATIONAL SOURCING DATABASE http://wwigner.cped.orni.gov/nsbd. Integrates several data sources with information on companies producing apparel items, textile and fabric products, machinery and equipment.

NSPA (NORTHWEST SEWN PRODUCTS ASSOCIATION) 147 S.E. 102nd St., Portland, OR 97216; 503-261-1926; Fax 503-253-9385; www.nwsewn.com. A nonprofit association for the textile, apparel and other sewn products industries of the Pacific Northwest.

SAN FRANCISCO FASHION INDUSTRIES (SFFI) 1000 Brannan St., Ste. 206, San Francisco, CA 94103; 415-621-6100; Fax 415-621-6384; www.sffi.org. The membership in this industry organization consists of manufacturers, suppliers, production services and professional services in the Bay Area. They will provide information on the phone to help you locate who and what you need. Their directory is published in February and August of each year.

SOUTHEASTERN APPAREL MANUFACTURERS AND SUPPLIERS ASSOCIATION (SEAMS) 1900 Broad River Rd., Ste. 10,0 Columbia, SC 29210-7047; 803-772-5861; www.seams.org. A nonprofit organization of garment manufacturers and suppliers in the southeastern U.S. working for the survival of the domestic sewn products industry by providing referrals, consultations, benefits packages, training and lobbying.

TALA (THE TEXTILE ASSOCIATION OF LOS ANGELES) 110 E. Ninth St., Ste. C765, Los Angeles, CA 90079; 213-627-6173; www.talausa.com. Because L.A. is the major garment-producing area in the country, there are many resources, sources, suppliers, etc., located in or near the city. This group will give you information over the phone about where to locate a specific fabric. Their information is almost always for West Coast sources and mainly in the L.A. area. They also publish a printed and CD-ROM directory annually: $100 each.

TECHNOLOGY EXCHANGE Imagine That! Consulting Group, Inc., 2229 Sherwood Ct., Minnetonka, MN 55305; 952-593-9085; www.techexchange.com. Searchable databases of software and hardware, consultants, service bureaus for the apparel, textile and home furnishings industries.

TEXTILE WEB (Information available online only.) 336-218-8562; www.textileweb.com. A vertical online marketplace—fabric show and other information services—for industry professionals.

Fabric Shows and Garment Manufacturing Shows

FOR CURRENT LISTINGS AND INFORMATION, CHECK THE TRADE SHOW CALENDAR AT WWW.APPAREL-NEWS.NET.

BOBBIN SHOWS 800-789-2223; www.vnuexpo.com and www.bobbin.com. (970 exhibitors—which is very large). Every three years on the East coast. Equipment, apparel-specific software and hardware, some fabrics and trims, etc. Geared to larger manufacturers; definitely worth attending to see what is happening at the cutting edge.

FABRIC TRIM AND FIBER (FTF) (Executive Events LLC) Portland, OR. 503-228-9647; www.eeventz.com. Fabrics, leathers & other sportswear/activewear-related products. Spring and Fall: Portland, OR.

FASHION TECHNOLOGY BY DESIGN (California Fashion Association and California Technology Trade and Commerce, Los Angeles, CA) 213-688-6288. Primarily apparel specific software, seminars.

INTERNATIONAL FASHION FABRIC EXHIBITION (IFFE) 800-421-9567; www.magiconline.com. Jacob Javits Center, New York City. Fall and Spring.

INTERNATIONAL TEXTILES AND SEWING PRODUCTS EXPO 516-596-3937; textileshow@earthlink.net. Wholesale fabrics and trim to fabric and craft stores and small manufacturers. Spring and Fall shows in Las Vegas.

LOS ANGELES INTERNATIONAL TEXTILE SHOW (CaliforniaMart and TALA) 800-CAL-MART; www.californiamart.com. Spring and Fall shows at California Mart.

MATERIAL WORLD MIAMI BEACH (Urban Expositions, Marietta, GA) 678-285-3976; www.fairchildexpo.com.

NAMSB WORLDSOURCE 212-685-4550; www.nambsworldsource.com. International apparel and textiles. Fall in New York City.

NORTHWEST APPAREL AND FOOTWEAR MATERIALS SHOW (American Classic Events) 503-642-0977; ntrlshow@aol.com., www.americanevents.com. Fabrics, leathers and other sportswear/activewear-related products. Spring and Fall; Portland, OR.

SEWN PRODUCTS EXPO 800-765-7615; www.vnuexpo.com. Bi-annually in the Spring in Los Angeles. Equipment, apparel-specific software and hardware, some fabrics and trims, etc. Geared to larger manufacturers; definitely worth seeing.

SURTEX (George Little Management) 800-272-SHOW; www.glmshows.com.

Trade Shows—As An Exhibitor

CHECK THE TRADE SHOW CALENDAR AT WWW.APPARELNEWS.NET. THERE ARE NUMEROUS OTHER SHOWS. AS YOU PROCEED WITH YOUR BUSINESS YOU WILL BECOME FAMILIAR WITH THE MOST APPROPRIATE VENUES FOR YOUR PRODUCTS.

ACTION SPORTS RETAILER Long Beach and San Diego, CA; 800-486-6508; www.asrbiz.com.

ACCESSORIES THE SHOW 800-358-6678; Several times a year in New York City.

DOUGLAS TRADE SHOWS Kaneohe, HI; 800-525-5275; www.douglastradeshows.com.

ECO EXPO Anaheim, CA and Washington, DC; 800-334-3976; www.ecoexpo.com.

FAME (Fashion Avenue Market Expo) 877-904-3263; www.fameshows.com. Women's apparel and accessories, New York City.

FASHIONMART@SAN FRANCISCO GIFT CENTER 415-861-7733; www.sfgiftcenter.com.

GEORGE LITTLE MANAGEMENT (SURTEX, VISUAL MARKETING and GIFT SHOWS) 800-272-SHOW; www.glmshows.com.

GOLDEN GATE APPAREL ASSOCIATION San Francisco, CA; 925-328-1122; www.fashionsanfrancisco.com.

IMPRINTED SPORTSWEAR SHOWS Long Beach, CA and Tampa, FL; 800-527-0207; www.isshows.com.

MAGIC INTERNATIONAL 800-421-9567; www.magiconline.com. A huge series of shows held in February and August in Las Vegas: MAGIC, WWDMAGIC (Women), MAGICKids and THE EDGE. Shows held in New York City in Spring and Fall: INTERNATIONAL FASHION BOUTIQUE SHOW, STYLE INDUSTRIE FEMME, INTERNATIONAL KIDS FASHION SHOW.

NEW ENGLAND APPAREL CLUB Westwood, MA; 781-326-9223. Five shows per year in Boston area.

THE NEW NAMSB SHOW (NNS) NSI New York, NY; 800-936-2672; www.nsi-shows.com. Men and boys apparel and shoes; Spring and Fall: Javits Center.

OUTDOOR RETAILER 800-486-2701; www.outdoorretailer.com.

PACIFIC NORTHWEST APPAREL ASSOCIATION Seattle, WA; 206-767-9200; pnaa@earthlink.net.

SOUTHERN APPAREL EXHIBITORS Ladies and children's apparel and accessories show. Miami, FL; 888-249-1377; www.floridafashionfocus.com.

SPECIALTY SHOWS B.A.T. (Big & Tall Woman), B.A.T. Man, and Intimate Apparel Show. 305-663-6635; www.spectrade.com.

SURF EXPO Orlando, FL; 800-947-SURF; www.surfexpo.com.

U.S. Regional Apparel Markets and Marts

ATLANTA
AMC, Inc. AmericasMart
240 Peachtree St., Ste. 2200
Atlanta, GA 30303
888-262-6309
www.americasmart.com

BIRMINGHAM
Birmingham Apparel Market
Bessemer Civic Center
Bessemer, AL
205-871-3305

BOSTON
New England Apparel Club
Royal Plaza Trade Center & Hotel Show
Marlboro, MA
781-326-9223
800-272-6972, 612-333-5219

CHARLOTTE
Charlotte Apparel Mart/Merchandise Mart
2500 E. Independence Blvd.
Charlotte, NC 28205
704-333-7709
www.charlottemerchmart.com

CHICAGO
Chicago Apparel Club
Merchandise Mart
200 World Trade Center Chicago
Chicago, IL 60654
800-677-6278, 312-527-7600
www.mmart.com

DALLAS
International Apparel Mart
2300 Stemmons Freeway
Dallas, TX 75258
800-DAL-MKTS, 214-655-6100
www.dallasmarketcenter.com

DENVER
Denver Merchandise Mart
451 E. 58th Ave., #470
Denver, CO 80216-1422
800-289-6278, 303-292-6278
www.denvermart.com

KANSAS CITY
Kansas City Market Center
1775 Universal Ave., Ste. 1700
Kansas City, MO 64120
800-241-5510, 816-231-6446
www.visitkc.com

LOS ANGELES
California Mart
110 East Ninth St.
Los Angeles, CA 90007
213-630-3689
www.californiamart.com

MIAMI
Miami International Merchandise Mart
777 N.W. 72nd Ave.
Miami, FL 33126
800-333-3333, 305-261-2900

MINNEAPOLIS
Minneapolis Apparel Mart
Hyatt Merchandise Mart
1300 Nicolette Mall, Ste. 4052
Minneapolis, MN 55403

NEW YORK
Fashion Center Headquarters
249 W. 39th St.
New York, NY 10018
212-764-9600
www.fashioncenter.com

PITTSBURGH
Pittsburgh Expo Center
105 Mall Blvd.
Monroeville, PA 15146
888-366-4660
www.pittsburghfashionmart.com

SALT LAKE CITY
Salt Lake City Fashion Exhibitors Mart
230 W. 200 S.
Salt Lake City, UT 84101
801-531-6699

SAN FRANCISCO
Golden Gate Apparel Association
12925 Alcosta Blvd., Ste. 7
San Ramon, CA 94583
925-328-1122
www.fashionsanfrancisco.com

SEATTLE
Seattle Trends Show
Stadium Exhibition Center
1000 Occidental Ave.
Seattle, WA 98134
206-767-9200
pnaa@earthlink.net

118

APPENDIX C: FORMS

Income Statement

	JAN	FEB	MAR	APR	MAY	JUN
INCOME						
Sales						
Freight						
Other						
Total Income						
COST OF GOODS						
Material						
Trims						
Labor						
Patterns						
Other						
Total COG						
GROSS PROFIT						
EXPENSES						
Advertising						
Bank Charges						
Car Expenses						
Dues						
Education						
Equipment Rental						
Entertainment						
Legal/Professional						
Office Supplies						
Permits/Licenses						
Printing						
Postage						
Photography						
Publications						
Rent						
Shipping						
Storage						
Telephone						
Trade Shows						
Utilities						
Total Expenses						
NET INCOME						

Income Statement, continued

	JUL	AUG	SEP	OCT	NOV	DEC	TOTAL
INCOME							
Sales							
Freight							
Other							
Total Income							
COST OF GOODS							
Material							
Trims							
Labor							
Patterns							
Other							
Total COG							
GROSS PROFIT							
EXPENSES							
Advertising							
Bank Charges							
Car Expenses							
Dues							
Education							
Equipment Rental							
Entertainment							
Legal/Professional							
Office Supplies							
Permits/Licenses							
Printing							
Postage							
Photography							
Publications							
Rent							
Shipping							
Storage							
Telephone							
Trade Shows							
Utilities							
Total Expenses							
NET INCOME							

Confidential Disclosure Agreement

Letters like these can be found in books of forms in county law libraries.

SAMPLE 1

RE: (Your Design or Product Name)

The ideas, designs and concepts, which are being disclosed and discussed today, are being disclosed to you in the strictest confidence. You hereby acknowledge (1) that all of the said information, designs and concepts are the property of <u>(Your name/company)</u>; (2) that you are receiving said information in confidence; and (3) that you will not disclose any of the ideas, designs, concepts or information to others or use them yourself in whole or in part for any purpose without the prior written consent of <u>(Your name/company name)</u>.

I have read this Confidential Disclosure Agreement and agree to its terms.

_____   _____

<u>(Name of party reviewing your designs &/or goods)</u>   <u>(Date)</u>

SAMPLE 2

<u>(Name of party reviewing your designs &/or goods)</u> will not at any time, in any fashion or manner, whether directly or indirectly, divulge, disclose, or communicate to any person, firm, or corporation in any manner whatsoever any information of any kind, nature, or description concerning any matters affecting or relating to any or all of the designs or samples of <u>(Your name/company name)</u>, her manner of operation, or her plans, processes or other data of any kind, nature, or description without regard to whether any or all of the foregoing matters would be deemed confidential, material or important.

The parties hereby stipulate that as between them the foregoing matters are important, material, proprietary, trade secrets and confidential, and gravely affect the effective and successful conduct of <u>(Your name/company name)</u> and her goodwill, and that any breach of the terms of this section is a material breach of this agreement.

_____   _____

<u>(Name of party reviewing your designs &/or goods)</u>   <u>(Date)</u>

_____

<u>Your name</u>

Market Research Form

A. DEMOGRAPHICS Who is your ideal customer? Be as specific as you can. Do your research at stores and trade shows and by asking friends. Then target your market—the people to whom you will be selling. All characteristics may not be relevant for you, or you may need to include others.

Characteristics   **Findings/Source**
1) Age
2) Sex
3) Marital Status
4) Occupation
5) Geographic Location
6) Other

B. LIFESTYLE & PERSONALITY Are they important to defining your ideal customer? Today, people buy products not just because they need them but because buying makes them feel better about themselves, a cause, or an idea in which they believe.

Characteristics   **Findings/Source**
1) Buying Habits
2) Lifestyle
3) Personality
4) Leisure Time
5) Other

C. BENEFITS What benefits does your product have for your customer? You must be very clear and specific here. For example, you cannot provide high quality and sell at a low price. Find your benefits, stay focused and develop products that achieve these benefits.

Benefits   **Findings/Source**
1) Price
2) Quality
3) Style
4) Uniqueness
5) Fabrication
6) Other

D. INFLUENTIAL FACTORS What factors will influence current and future market trends? You cannot design and manufacture in a "vacuum." It is essential to your business that you know and can tell potential buyers how your product fits into current and future market trends.

Factors   **Findings/Source**
1) Economy
2) Location/Traffic
3) Seasonality
4) Technology
5) Sociocultural Influences
6) Trade Laws
7) Other

E. COMPETITIVE ANALYSIS Studying/working into and around your competition. You must know who your competition is by name, product category and, if possible, market share. You will use this information to tell potential buyers why they need to buy your product.

Factors   Findings/Source

1) Who are your competitors?
2) What is their share of the market?
3) What are their perceived strengths and weaknesses?
4) Is the market overloaded or is there room for more?
5) Other

F. WRITE YOUR POSITIONING STATEMENT After completing your analysis you will have a clear, focused vision of what your product is, who your ideal customer is and how your product will benefit them. Now you are ready to write your positioning statement. In 7 to 10 words state why your product or service has value and why it should be purchased. This statement may develop into your slogan and will be used to introduce your company and product to potential buyers.

Your Positioning Statement:_____

_____

_____

Initial Design Spec Sheet

Date:_____

Design Sketch and Fabrics
StyleName:_____ **Prototype #:**_____

Season: _____ Delivery Date:_____ Size Range:_____

Offered in What Colors/Fabrics:_____

_____

_____

Notes/Comments:_____

_____

_____

Fabric/Trim Spec Sheet

Date: _____

SWATCHES

Vendor Name/Phone/Fax: _____

_____

_____

Fabric/Trim Name: _____

Fiber Content: _____

Fabric/Trim Price: _____ **Fabric Width:** _____

Color Names/Numbers: _____

_____

_____

Lead Times/Minimum Orders: _____

_____

_____

Fabric/Trim Care: _____

_____

Other Notes: _____

_____

_____

_____

Apparel Industry Contractor Agreement

THIS FORM IS THE PROPERTY OF THE NORTHERN CALIFORNIA CHINESE GARMENT CONTRACTORS ASSOCIATION, THE CHINESE BAY AREA APPAREL CONTRACTORS ASSOCIATION AND SAN FRANCISCO FASHION INDUSTRIES. THIS FORM IS NOT TO BE REPRODUCED IN ANY WAY. IT IS AN EXAMPLE OF A LEGAL CONTRACTOR'S AGREEMENT.

Instructions: This Schedule must be completed in full and signed by both Parties before any of the Contracted Work listed hereon is to be performed by the Contractor. Please attach to this Schedule any duly executed additional agreements between the parties.

Name and Address of Company / Name and Address of Contractor:_____

_____

Identifying Information, Notice Periods and Delivery Dates

Agreement #:_____

Delivery date for fabric, trim, etc., to be delivered to Contractor: _____, 20___.

Agreed completion date for Contracted Work: _____, 20___.

Agreed period for Contractor to notify Company of need for overtime work following notice of
completion deadline/delay (minimum 2 days):_____days.

Agreed period for recision of this Agreement: _____days.

Company must approve completed sample before Contracted Work begins? Yes _____ No___

The Contracted Work

1. Price per unit: $_____ Style #: _____ Cut #:_____

2. The type of contracted work (check all that are applicable):

    __sewing   __ cutting __ pressing   __ trimming   __ tagging   __ folding

    __ bundling   __ poly-bagging   __ pickup and delivery __ quality control   __ other

*Please specify "other":*_____

   Note: This entry must include all significant labor operations or services to be performed by the contractor.

3. Total number of contracted pieces: _____

4. (Optional) Agreed proportional progress payments (check one)

       __ weekly   __ biweekly   __ other

Apparel Industry Contractor Agreement, continued 2

Amount Due Contractor

A. Total basic payment due: $_____ *(Multiply price per unit in line 1 by pieces in line 3, above.)*

   Note: Calculate all labor work at regular wage rates; include below online B any allowance for overtime wages and other expenses.

B. Agreed repair/rework percentage allowance to Contractor:_____% = $_____.

C. Initial agreed overtime wage allowance to Contractor: $_____.

D. Grand total due to Contractor for all Contracted Work: $_____.

   (Add Lines A, B and C above.)

The Parties hereby agree that each Party shall have three (3) working days (or a shorter period agreed upon above) after it executes this Agreement to review the amounts due to Contractor listed on this Agreement, and either Party may rescind this Schedule during that period without cost or obligation.

(Company)   (Contractor)
By: _____   By: _____
Title: _____   Title: _____
Date:_____   Date: _____

ADDENDA (To be agreed upon after execution of Schedule A)

1. Agreed extension of completion date to new date: _____

   (Requires Company approval.)

   Initials of Parties: Company {   } Contractor {   } Date: _____

2. Agreed sums to be paid to Contractor for additional overtime expense and other expenses that are due to company-imposed delay or completion deadline: $_____

   (Requires Company approval.)

   Initials of Parties: Company {   } Contractor {   } Date: _____

Contractor's Certification of Compliance With Wage and Hour Laws

THIS FORM IS THE PROPERTY OF THE NORTHERN CALIFORNIA CHINESE GARMENT CONTRACTORS ASSOCIATION, THE CHINESE BAY AREA APPAREL CONTRACTORS ASSOCIATION AND SAN FRANCISCO FASHION INDUSTRIES. THIS FORM IS NOT TO BE REPRODUCED IN ANY WAY. IT IS AN EXAMPLE OF A LEGAL CONTRACTOR'S AGREEMENT.

Contractor #: _____

Contractor Name: _____Telephone #: _____

Contractor Address: _____

City: _____State: _____ Zip Code: _____

Contractor California Registration No. (per Labor Code Sec. 2675): _____

Expiration date of registration: _____

Cut #: _____Style #: _____

Applicable Agreement #: (See applicable Agreement) _____

Date Completed Contract Work was delivered to Company_____

I,_____, certify that:
    (Print Name)

1. I am authorized by the above-named Contractor to make this certification on its behalf.

2. The goods produced pursuant to the above-referenced Contract, were completed in compliance with all applicable state and federal wage and hour laws.

Dated: _____   _____
                                                       (Contractor's Signature)

                                               _____
                                                    (Print Name and Title)

Contractor Profile and Evaluation Form

Today's Date:_____   Owner/Contact Name:_____
Factory Name:_____   # of Employees:_____
Street Address:_____   In Business Since:_____
City/State/Zip:_____   Garment Mfr's License #:_____
Phone:_____   Garment Mfr's License Exp. Date:_____
Fax:_____   Compliance Codes:_____
Email:_____   Liability Insurance:_____

Services Provided In-house

	Yes/No	Notes
Pattern Making		
First Sample		
Grading		
Trim Purchasing		
Care Label Printing		
Screen Printing		
Embroidery		
Snap Setting		
Buttonhole/Button Sew		

Sewing

	Yes/No	Notes
Knits		
Wovens		
Jackets		
Swimwear		
Denim		
Home Furnishings		
Budget, Moderate		
Bridge, Couture		
Factory Specializes In		

Cutting

	Yes/No	Notes
Knits		
Wovens		

Contractor Profile and Evaluation Form, continued 2

Factory Name:_____ **Today's Date:**_____

Packaging

	Yes/No	Notes
Poly Bag		
Garment On Hanger (GOH)		
Prepacks		
Hand Iron		
Buck Press		

Communication & Organization

	Yes/No	Notes
English-Speaking Proficiency		
English-Writing Proficiency		
Fax Machine		
Computer Systems		
Client Meeting Area		
Factory Cleanliness		

Documentation

	Yes/No	Notes
Use Labor Price Quote Sheet		
Use Cut/Purchase Order Sheet		
Use Product Spec Sheet		
Use Approval Samples		
Use Packing Slips		

Raw Materials & Processing

	Yes/No	Notes
Verifies Incoming Fabric		
Adequate Fabric Storage		
Does Fabric Pre-Inspection		
Trim Verification & Storage		

Contractor Profile and Evaluation Form, continued 3

Factory Name:_____ **Today's Date:**_____

Inspection

	Yes/No	Notes
Uses Formal QC/QA Program		
Does In-Line Inspections		
Does Final Inspections		
Supervisor/Operator Ratio (Best: 1 to 20 or less)		

Costing

	Yes/No	Notes
Based on Breakdown Calculations		
Based on SAMs		
Based on Quantity of P.O.		
Based on Client Record		
Uses Operator Incentives		

Cost Sheet

Date:_____

Season:_____

Style Name:_____

Style Number:_____

Fabrics/Trim: Prices per yard or unit ordered

_____

_____

_____

_____

A. Fabric Name/cost per item (from above)

Fabric   _____

Fabric   _____

Lining   _____

Interfacing   _____

Other   _____

Total Materials Cost_____

B. Trims/cost per item (from above)

Buttons   _____

Zippers   _____

Elastic   _____

Patch/label   _____

Bias/cording   _____

Other   _____

Total Trims Cost_____

C. Cutting Cost per item   _____

D. Sewing Cost per item   _____

Total Cut & Sew Cost_____

E. Other Costs   _____

F. Packaging   _____

G. FIRST COST (Add lines A-F) _____

H. WHOLESALE COST   _____

    Line G x Markup%   _____

I. SUGGESTED RETAIL

    Line H x Markup%   _____

Sketch and Fabric

place sketch & fabric
swatches for style here

Check List For Trade Shows

All side drapes and table covers must be fire retardant. Fire marshals will check your display for fire-retardancy. Any drapes or table covers supplied by the promoters of your shows will meet fire-retardancy standards. There are fabric suppliers who specialize in fire retardant fabrics.

DISPLAY

____Samples to be displayed.

____Samples for the buyers to touch and look at closely.

____Swatches of fabrications or colors not shown in samples.

____Samples of actual size—important in childrenswear & accessories.

____Display props—photos, decorations, balloons, etc.

____Table covers & drapes—if the show provides them they will be overpriced and tacky; bring your own.

____Push pins	____Silver tape	____Scissors
____Straight	____Tissue paper	____Pliers
____Assorted safety	____Steamer	

____A sheet or large piece of fabric to close off your booth at night to help reduce the likelihood of sticky fingers making off with your samples—in spite of the show's security personnel.

SELLING

____PR materials—mounted copies of press coverage, for example.

____Line sheets

____Order forms

____Business cards

____Printing calculator

PORTABLE OFFICE

____Hand-held mini cassette recorder for making memos needing attention when you return your office; those paper notes have a way of getting lost in the mad dash to pack up and get out.

____Laptop computer, if you have one and have need and/or plan to be online to e-mail orders to your home office. You can rent a phone line at the show for e-mail and Internet access.

____Cell phone and or pager, if you have one and have need to be in constant contact with your home office. You can also rent a phone line and phone at the show.

____Palm™ handheld or similar organizer to manage, share and secure information.

____Paper clips	____Pens and pencils
____Stapler	____Note pad

Sales Rep Agreement

Dear _____,

This letter is intended to outline the terms under which you will represent _____ as an Independent Sales Representative. This contract starts on _____ and will continue for 6 months ending _____. At that time the contract will be reviewed for an additional 12 months and will be renewable annually from that time on. This contract is cancelable if either party gives the other party a 60-day notice.

Territory

Your territory will include the following states:

This applies to specialty stores and major stores written in this area. The majors and catalogs in your territory include:

If another independent representative works your account at a market or in his/her territory, you will split your commission with that independent representative.

Sales Commissions

Commissions are paid on net-shipped volume (gross shipping less returns and allowances). The commission rate for full-price sales is____%. The commission rate for off-price and discounts is____%. Commissions are paid the last day of the month for payments received that month.

Sales Samples

Each season you will be shipped a line of samples for all styles for that season. You will be invoiced for these samples at a 50% discount from wholesale price. This sample invoice will be due after that particular season has shipped (netted against commissions for that particular season).

Accepted and Agreed

By_____   By_____

   (sales rep's printed name)   (company owner's printed name)

_____   _____

          (signature)   (signature)

Date_____   Date_____

Purchase Order/Cut-Sew Ticket

Date: _____

To: _____   From: _____

Style #: _____ P.O.#: _____   P.O. Due Date: _____

Sizes

Color # and Name	XS/2	S/4	M/6	L/8	XL/10	12	TOTAL
TOTAL:							

Total Cut Units: _____   Unit Costs: _____   Total Cost: _____

Total Sewn Units: _____   Unit Costs: _____   Total Cost: _____

Signed by: _____

Special Requirements/Comments:

1.

2.

3.

Quality Control Sheet

VENDOR:_____STYLE #:_____

DESCRIPTION OF ITEM BEING EVALUATED:_____
_____

This completed form due back to production with first shipment.

SPECIFICATIONS:
(If garment is treated in any way that will affect sizing, please submit these as final specs to the in-house production manager. Also, please note under "washing Instructions" the shrinkage percentage of this garment.)

Specifications	S/2	M/4	L/6	XL/8	10	12	14
Chest							
Waist							
Hips							
Inseam Length							
Outseam Length							
Front rise							
Back rise							
Neck to waist (front)							
Neck to waist (back)							
Shoulder to shoulder							
Sleeve length							

WASHING INSTRUCTIONS:
(If garment specifications change as a result of the washing/drying process, include new washing instructions as they *should* read on care label. Also include any shrinkage information as per above.)
_____
_____

CHANGES, REVISIONS, SPECIAL INSTRUCTIONS: _____
_____
_____

Independent Contractor Agreement

This agreement is entered into this day of _____, 20_____

between_____and _____.

             (manufacturer/company name)   (contractor name)

The parties agree as follows:

1. You will cut the garments out of the fabric I have provided with the patterns I have provided and sew the garments to my specifications. I will provide all fabrics, trim and accessories required to complete each garment.

2. You will be paid by the piece at the agreed-upon price written on each garment P.O.

3. You are responsible for all expenses, personnel, tools, and equipment beyond the materials I will provide, including any repairs needed to fully perform these services.

4. You are responsible for all payroll, income and unemployment tax deductions/payments due to these services because I am not your employer.

5. You shall carry, at your cost, during this contract all necessary workers' compensation insurance covering you and your employees, as well as general liability insurance.

6. You shall fully comply with all the applicable federal, state and local laws and regulations during the time of this contract.

7. You shall keep all information about my business confidential, including designs and ideas, disclosing them to no one without my express written consent.

8. As an independent contractor, you agree that I retain the right to visit your work area at any time during operating hours, unannounced, to observe the production of my garments.

9. All work will be performed within your factory unless otherwise noted and agreed upon by me.

10.This agreement is the entire agreement, with/without attachments, and may be amended or altered only in writing, signed by both parties. The laws of the State of California govern this agreement.

By_____   By_____

        (manufacturer/company name)   (contractor name)

Production Spec Sheet

Date:_____

Company Name:_____Deliveries: _____

Style:_____Sizes:_____

Phone:_____Contact Person:_____

Style Name:	Trims	Quantity	Size	Color	Supplier
	buttons				
	snaps				
	zippers				
	elastic				
place sketch of style here	**Fabrics**	**Quantity**	**Content**	**Describe**	**Supplier**
	base				
	base				
	base				
	lining				
Fabric Consumption:	lining				

COLOR CHART

Style#	Body Color	Trim Color	Lining Color	Other	Button Color	Zipper Color	Label ID	Other

Attach Fabric and Trim Swatches in Space Below

APPENDIX D: BUSINESS PLAN

COZY TOPS OF CALIFORNIA

1000 MAIN STREET

ANY TOWN, CA 00000-0000

800-000-0000 FAX 800-100-0000

BUSINESS PLAN

BY LEE LEVIN

JANUARY 1, 2020

Business Plan Table of Contents

A. General Overview
    1. Legal Structure
    2. Business Type
    3. Market Opportunity
B. Product Description
    1. Line Description
    2. Unique Selling Properties
    3. Line Sheet
C. Market Description
    1. Demographics
    2. Lifestyle and Personality
    3. Influential Factors
    4. Competitive Analysis
D. Marketing and Sales Plan
    1. Marketing Concept
    2. Sales Plan
    3. Advertising Plan
E. Design Development and Production Plan
    1. Design Plan
    2. Production Plan
    3. Shipping Plan
    4. Accounting Plan
F. Financial Data
    1. Start-Up Cash Plan
    2. Year 1 Projections
    3. Year 2 Projections
    4. Year 3 Projections
G. Supporting Documents
    1. Line Sheet
    2. Cost Sheet
    3. Production Spec Sheet
    4. Fabric/Trim Spec Sheet
    5. Income Statement Years 1-3
    6. Personal Resume

A. General Overview

Legal Structure

COZY TOPS is a sole proprietorship run and operated by Lee Levin. I have chosen this legal structure because at this time I intend to make all the design, manufacturing and sales decisions for my company. Because this is my first independent business venture, I have chosen the business structure that is the easiest and least expensive to establish and that will give me total control of my company's growth. I project that in two to five years I will change my business structure to a corporation as my product distribution and, therefore, company liability increases.

Business Type

The type of business I will conduct is garment manufacturing of infant/toddler hats and accessories. My experience for five years as a design assistant to an infant-clothing manufacturer has allowed me the opportunity to understand the manufacturing process. I will design my products by producing sketches and rough prototypes. I will then work with a local patternmaker and sample sewer to produce my selling samples. Initially, I will be responsible for selling my product line. I plan to contact the specialty and department stores where I see my product selling and make a presentation to each buyer. This firsthand sales exposure will allow me to hear all the feedback on my line and adapt it, if I can, to make the sale. As my product is accepted into more wholesale accounts, I plan to locate sales reps to take on the selling responsibility.

Market Opportunity

This is an opportune time for my business venture for two primary reasons. First, Any Town is located in the San Francisco Bay area, where I will tap into the many available entrepreneurial garment-manufacturing services for producing my products. I have developed relationships with many of these patternmakers, graders and sewing contractors through my past employment. Second, I feel the market is hot for high-quality fashion hats and accessories for the infant/toddler set that are original and well made and evoke a mood of fun and fantasy. The uniqueness of my product will come from whimsical fabrics, novel color mixes and original designs.

B. Product Description

Line Description

The product line of COZY TOPS consists of hats, booties and matching bibs for the infant and toddler set. Fabrics will be machine-washable 100% cotton seersuckers and bold bright prints for summer, with cotton-blended plaids, checks, flannels and corduroys for fall and winter. Designed specifically with the infant in mind (the largest size is 24 months/Preschool) my company's styles are both highly functional—to protect babies from the sun— and whimsically charming. When possible, hats and bibs are reversible to allow added versatility.

Initially, there will be 4 hat silhouettes, 1 bib style and 1 bootie style that will be offered year-round in a wide variety of appropriate fabric weights and colors. The idea is the customer will enjoy the fit and quality of my products, which will remain constant, and I will change the colors, prints and textures as the season and my design instinct demand. All items are designed to be purchased separately so the customers can match solids and prints as they choose. All items will have a hangtag on them to describe their versatility and list the other products that can be purchased to go with them. Items will wholesale from $8 for bibs to $14 for hats and booties.

Designed into my product is the year-round need for constant basic colors; novelty prints and stripes are offered on a seasonal basis. Designing this way, I can always keep my line appearing fresh and new and fulfill the various color and print requests of my customers. I may offer a lower price structure for my basics and a higher price for my novelties. I plan to embroider my "sun" logo onto my products. I feel brand identification is very important, and I want my customers to be able to identify my product wherever they travel.

Unique Selling Features

Function, versatility and attention to detail are what make my products unique. All booties will be flannel-lined for warmth and have a no-skid rubber bottom to aid in walking and prevent slipping. All hats will have extra-wide brims and flaps to keep the sun off the infant's neck and face. The bibs will tie around the infant's neck to allow for ease in putting on and removing. Although I offer pastel and primary colors, my goal is to make a unisex product that promotes the joy of childhood.

C. Market Description

Demographics

The demographics of my customer are quite different from the demographics of the ultimate wearer of my product, the child. My ideal customers will be parents, grandparents and friends of the parents, grandparents or child. The age of my customer will be from twenty on up. My product will appeal to men and women, but I anticipate mostly women will buy it. Marital status is not significant. Occupations will vary greatly and should not affect purchasing. My product is in the moderate to high price range and will be affordable to those with middle to high income. The geographic location of my customer will vary mostly by climate zones. Although my products are offered year round, my winter hats and booties are designed for mild winters, not those of the Midwest and northeastern United States.

Lifestyle and Personality

My customers are practical yet have a sense of style and whimsy. They are not afraid to accessorize an outfit with a wild animal print, black polka dots or oversized floral prints. Some of my customers will still be drawn to pastel colors for girls and primary colors for boys, but the majority will enjoy the diversity of product I offer. Their personalities are lively and upbeat. They appreciate the value of 100% cotton products for their children and want to provide year round sun protection. Some of their buying behavior will be impulse purchases—what most of us do when we see just the right thing. Some of their buying habits will be repeat purchases as their children grow or they buy baby gifts for friends and family members.

Influential Factors

The most influential trends that will affect the production of my products are the economic trends which always affect the garment manufacturing industry. I intend to produce my product domestically and hope I can continue to compete with products manufactured in areas of lower labor costs. Because there is growing awareness of human rights and some abuses in labor of the garment industry, I plan to advertise as a Made in America product. I think this will help justify the price of my products.

Another trend I am riding is one to keep infant faces, necks and ears covered to protect them from the sun's UV rays twelve months of the year. I feel the importance of this environmental trend will continue and my products will satisfy this need.

Competitive Analysis

My primary competition is from infant collections like Little Me, House of Hatten, Absorba, Sweet Potatoes and Mothers Maid. These infant collections generally offer hats included with the purchase of their sundresses, sunsuits and baby outfits. There are also companies whose main focus is hats, like Flap Happy, Bartholomew's and Carole Ampere. COZY TOPS will be unique in that we offer hats separately, without the clothing, and we have booties and bib to match all of the hats. Another form of competition is from private-label lines that department stores carry. I plan to contact these department store buyers and produce a COZY TOPS private-label collection. The collection will consist of our silhouettes offered in special patterns and prints exclusively for each store.

D. Marketing and Sales Plan

Marketing Concept

COZY TOPS will be marketed with its own product identity. The stylized sun logo and company name will be used to identity all products. I have picked a clear sky-blue color for my logo because I feel it is peaceful and easy to read and will print well on white card stock. My logo will be used on my hangtags, labels, and order forms and in all paperwork dealing with my company. I feel that logo identification is very important for establishing a product in our competitive market. I will also embroider my logo on a line of basic signature hats, booties and bibs to help identify the product to all my customers when they are out strolling with their infants.

I will enter the market with my Spring 2021 collection and then will offer Summer, Fall and Holiday collections. Part of my sales and marketing plan for the first year is to establish my line with key accounts within a 200-mile radius of my headquarters in San Francisco. From looking in phone books and making initial sales calls, I project there are twenty good accounts that should carry my line. I will call accounts, set up appointments with the buyers and do a sales presentation in their stores. I plan to offer my accounts product photos and fabric swatches, as needed, to understand my seasonal collections and see the beauty of my products on an infant. In my first year, I also plan to travel to New York and Las Vegas to participate in the major kids trade shows. I feel this exposure is mandatory to establish my line. I have walked both of these shows within the past year to get a better idea of how to set up a booth and where my booth should be located at the shows. Before the shows, I will contact the major kids catalogs and department store buyers and invite them to visit my booth.

Sales Plan

In Years 2-5, I plan to add sales reps in key locations throughout the country. My current projection is New York, Atlanta, Florida, Texas, Los Angeles and San Francisco. I will supply photos of and signage for my products to my reps, along with line lists and other company promotion items to keep the presence of my line alive in their showrooms. I will supply them each with a seasonal sample line. I will continue to travel biannually to New York and Las Vegas to do the major Spring and Fall shows. I feel this is required to properly market and promote myself, my company's philosophy and my product.

Advertising Plan

Advertising will clearly help sell my product. I will have a website that advertises and promotes my products and lists accounts where COZY TOPS may be purchased. (Initially I will not accept retail sales via my site because I need to focus on maintaining my wholesale accounts. In the future I would consider selling retail via the Web.) In my first year I will rely on my product promoting itself with the line lists and photos I supply to my customers. I will, however, take out small cooperative ads (ads for which I share the cost with my stores, and we both advertise our names and promote our products) with select stores in newspapers that have proven to bring them business. I also will develop my customer mailing list. I feel direct mail is vital to keeping in touch with my customers and advising them of any promotions or specials I will be having.

More advertising will be required to maintain my presence in the marketplace in Years 2-5. I plan to place ads in appropriate show guides during market weeks to bring business to my sales reps' showrooms. I also will take out quarter-page ads in the major trade magazines—*Children's Business*, *Earnshaw's* and *Small World*—at the times of major shows. I will continue developing my mailing list and send direct-mail pieces to my wholesale customers. Via my website I will have developed a list of potential retail customers and will include them in my mailings.

I believe there are great possibilities for "free advertising." My product is colorful and adorable and looks outstanding on infants. I will be in contact with editors of magazines like *Parenting*, *Mothering* and *Child* to feature my products and use them in photo shoots. I will maintain a press kit to send to buyers. I will always contact them before shows and bring extra samples with me for potential photo shoots. I feel this type of advertising will be much more cost-effective than paying for an ad in a major magazine.

E. Design Development and Production Plan

Design Plan

I, Lee Levin, will be the head designer for COZY TOPS. I feel very qualified to handle this position, since I have been designing products for my past employer for five years and for my friends and me for most of my life. I plan to develop basic blocks for the baseball hats, floppy, full- brim sun hats and boating hats. I will subsequently design variations on these styles for all seasons and sizes. For the bib and booties, which are more basic, I will work with existing styles or patterns in the market and rework them to my fit and design details. After sewing my first prototypes, I will fit them on the heads and feet of several children. I plan to work with a patternmaker and sample sewer to develop my actual production patterns and sales samples. Again, my silhouettes will be simple; it is the color matches and fabrics that will make my designs come alive.

I plan to design and sample four collections a year. My lines for Spring/Summer and Fall/Holiday will be similar; the basic differences will be in fabrication. Year round, my booties will be lined in a soft flannel in colors to match the hats and bibs. Year round, my bibs will have an absorbent batting to absorb drools. For Spring/Summer I will offer cotton prints and solids combined in interesting ways. For Fall/Holiday I will add corduroys, flannels and chambray. I believe one of my biggest challenges will be locating fabrics I like. I plan to work with fabric jobbers as much as possible to obtain better selection and pricing for my fabrics. I also will work with several well-established mills for my basic fabrics where I will need larger quantities on a continual basis. I may need to travel to the fabric shows in Las Vegas or Los Angeles biannually to find exactly what I am looking for.

Production Plan

I will contract out all production cutting and sewing. I have relationships with several contractors who are willing to work with start-up manufacturers. Initially, I will ship to, and store fabrics in, my office and deliver them to the cutter as needed. I plan to cut only after receiving orders. I will keep a production log sheet on Excel to keep track of what I need to produce by style/color/size. I will be responsible for developing cut-sew tickets, delivering and picking up production. I will provide the contractors with my spec sheets, pattern and prototype for each cut. I anticipate that even with this information, I will still need to do quality control work upon pickup.

Shipping Plan

For the first year I plan to pack, ship and store production in my garage, using for storage the boxes in which my goods are returned from the contractor. I will use UPS as my primary shipper and set up an account with them. I will include a computer-generated packing slip with all my shipments and send a copy of the invoice in the mail the day that I ship. In Years 2-5 I plan to relocate to another facility for storage, packing and shipping. There are many available storage centers that could be used for storage and shipping.

Design-Through-Shipping Calendar

From past experience I am familiar with the cycle of design/production/sales. I have included the calendar I plan to follow for my business. Because I am a start-up, I believe I will be able to adjust to the demands of quick response. However, because I am new, I feel I will also need the lead times of the traditional calendar to find my sales and give my contractors enough time to produce my products.

	DESIGN		SAMPLES		SELL		PRODUCE		SHIP	
	T	DD	T	DD	T	DD	T	DD	T	DD
FALL	1.1-2.28	1.1-6.30	2.15	2.15-7.15	3.15	3.15-7.31	5.1-7.15	5.1-8.15	6.30-9.30	6.30-10.15
HOLIDAY/RESORT	4.1-5.31	4.1-9:30	5.15	5.15-10.15	6.1-8.15	6.1-10.15	8.1-10.1	8.1-11.15	10.1-12.15	10.15-1.30
SPRING	7.5-8.31	7.1-12.30	8.15	8.15-1.15	9.1-11.1	9.1-1.15	11.1-1.15	11-2.15	1.30-3.31	1.30-4.30
SUMMER	11.1-12.15	11.1-4.30	11.15	11.15-4.15	1.1-1.31	1.1-5.15	2.15-4.15	2.15-6.1	4.15-5.31	4.15-6.15

T = Traditional Calendar **DD** = Dynamic Design   **Numbers** represent dates: 5.1 = May 1

Accounting Plan

I plan to set up credit terms with my vendors as soon as I receive approval from them. Many fabric manufacturers have 60-day terms, which will be of great help with my cash flow. I plan to ship all first-order specialty-store accounts C.O.D. and then offer Net 30 terms for future shipments. I am aware that most accounts pay past 30 days and I will set up a notification system for tracking past-due accounts.

With the aid of a software accounting package I will track all receivable and payables for the first year. In Years 2-5 I plan to hire a data entry person/bookkeeper to assist in my record keeping.

F. Financial Data

I have $100,000 to start my business; $60,000 has been accumulated through my savings and the remainder is a $40,000 interest-free loan from my relatives. I have the availability of my credit cards to help with cash flow. I do not plan to take out a bank loan at this time. My financial plan is conservative, but this is my first business venture and I want to see how I like working as an independent manufacturer without investing beyond my means. I will also be investing large amounts of my time in the business in the next years without taking a draw until my business can afford it. I currently own a computer and fax machine and am fluent in many computer programs, including Excel and QuickBooks, that I will use in my business. I have one dedicated phone line for my business and a small office space.

Year 1

I have included my operating plan forecast for my first year starting in July because I will only be working on one season, Spring. To meet the required target shipping dates of Jan/Feb for my first Spring season I will design and purchase sample fabrics and sales samples in July/August, sell my products in Sept/Oct and purchase production fabrics and do production in Nov/Dec. I am projecting the cost of goods for my first season on the basis of producing 3 hat styles, 1 bootie and 1 bib in 5 fabrications. I will sample the hats in 3 fabrics each and the booties and bibs in all fabrics. I will produce only one sample line my first season. I am projecting that my other expenses, including selling, will be lower these six months than in future seasons. This is based on my plan to target stores within a radius of San Francisco and not have major trade show expenses my first season.

My first-year sales are based on selling twenty accounts an average of 12 hats, 6 booties and 6 bibs. I feel this average assortment will give each store a good representation of my product. If my sales are stronger, I will be capable of producing more, since I will have stock on hand due to the large minimum requirements for some of my fabrics. I feel my projections are realistic for my product line.

I will not be receiving sales income for my first season until February 2021. My revenues are based on an average order of $1,000 for twenty accounts that I will begin to ship in January, with some orders being C.O.D. and others Net 30.

Year 2

My cost of goods for this year will increase greatly because I will be designing and producing two collections, Fall and Spring. I will still keep the size of my Fall line the same as Spring and plan to respond to customer feedback on fit and silhouette as best I can. To meet the required shipping dates of July/Aug for my first Fall season I will design and purchase sample fabrics and sales samples in Jan/Feb, sell my products in March/April and purchase production fabrics and do production in May/June. My Spring season schedule will be as described in Year 1, and it is, therefore, this year when I will have overlapping seasons. My sample costs are projected to be the same as Spring.

My selling expenses show the greatest increase because I will need to expand my base and attend one or two shows for Spring 2022. I project doing the Kids Show in New York and Las Vegas. I do not anticipate any major ad expenses this year. My line sheets, hangtags and photos will be sufficient.

My Year 2 sales show the same projection for Fall as Spring Year 1, and the largest increase for Spring 2022 will be when I attend a trade show and expand my customer base. I am projecting the same minimum order requirement but increasing my client base to 120 accounts.

Year 3

My cost of goods will increase greatly because I will be producing four complete collections: Spring, Summer, Fall and Holiday. I project I will add additional hat, bib and bootie styles and may add blankets and infant gift sets. I will again have costs for pattern development and my sampling will increase. I also project to add several sales reps this year, which will require producing a complete sample line for each rep.

My selling expenses will increase if I plan to attend two shows a season for Spring and Fall. I do not plan on attending shows for the smaller seasons of Summer and Holiday. I project that my sales reps will cover these seasons.

I plan to start an advertising campaign by taking out small ads in show bulletins and in local papers in areas where I have good accounts. My plan is to do co-op advertising where I can share the expenses with my sales reps and accounts. I plan to keep my accounts informed about my product line by mailing them closeout and reduced-price style lists. I do not plan on spending money for large color ads. I do plan on developing a press kit and keeping editors aware of my products and new line developments so they can photograph my product and use the photos in feature articles on a seasonal basis.

My Year 3 sales projections show a large increase. This is in response to offering four seasons a year and the projection that I will now have some department store and mail-order customers who will be purchasing in greater volume. My account base is now 150 stores, with 10% of them being department stores or catalog companies.

My cash flow will still be a challenge in Year 3. There will be some months when on paper I will show a profit but I will need the working capital to invest back into the business. I project I will have a continual profit in Year 5 and my cash flow will be more established. It is in Year 5 when I project I will take a draw on a regular basis.

G. Supporting Documents

Line Sheet

COZY TOPS

COZY TOPS
1000 Main Street
Any Town, CA 00000-0000
800-000-0000 Fax 800-100-0000
www.cozytops.com

Season: Spring 2201
Delivery: 1/30-3/30
Minimum Order: $200

Reversible Baseball Hat Style #10 **COST:** $9.00 **SIZES:** Small 0-6 months Medium 6-12 months Large 12-24 months Preschool 2-4 years	Our adorable 100% cotton hat is comfortable and cool. There is a surprise color inside each brim! This is a year-round favorite for all children on the go! **COLORS:** 100 Spring Fever 130 Dots 150 Stripes 10 White/logo embroidery 20 Black/logo embroidery
Back Flap Hat Style #12 **COST:** $11.00 **SIZES:** Smalll 0-6 months Medium 6-12 months Large 12-24 months Preschool 2-4 years	This hat is not only colorful and cute but also a great sun protector. The extended brim and back flap provide your children with the sun protection they need in a 100% cotton fabric. **COLORS:** 100 Spring Fever 130 Dots 150 Stripes 10 White/logo embroidery 20 Black/logo embroidery

✒All first orders are C.O.D. With credit approval reorders will be NET 30.
✒Any returns must be made within 10 days of receipt and with approval of our office.
✒5% discount on all prepaid orders.
✒A late charge of 1.5% per month is applied on all past-due accounts.
✒Special orders and private label available on request.

CozyTops   1000 Main Street   Any Town, CA   00000-0000   TEL 800-000-0000   FAX 800-100-0000

Cost Sheet

Date: *August 15, 2020*

Season: *Spring 2021*

Style Name: *Reversible Baseball Hat*

Style Number: *10*

Fabrics/Trim: Prices per yard or unit ordered

Dots & Stripes $4.50 per yard

A. Fabric Name/cost per item (from above)

Fabric	*Dots*	$1.50
Fabric		
Lining	*Stripes*	$1.50
Interfacing		.25
Other		
	Total Materials Cost	$3.25

B. Trims/cost per item (from above)

Buttons	.25
Zippers	
Elastic	.08
Patch/label	.07
Bias/cording	
Other	
Total Trims Cost	.40

C. Cutting Cost per item .50

D. Sewing Cost per item 1.55

Total Cut & Sew Cost 2.05

E. Other Costs

F. Packaging

G. FIRST COST (Add lines A-F) 5.70

H. WHOLESALE COST

　　　Line G x Markup% 11.40

I. SUGGESTED RETAIL

　　　Line H x Markup% 22.80

Sketch and Fabric

place sketch & fabric swatches for style here

Production Spec Sheet

Date: _November 15, 2020_

Company Name: _Cozy Tops_

Deliveries: _1/30/21.2/28/21.3/30/21_

Style: _# 10_

Sizes: _S, M, L, PS_

Phone: _800-000-0000_

Contact Person: _Lee Levin_

Style Name: Baseball Hat Reversible	Trims	Quantity	Size	Color	Supplier
	buttons	1	1/2"	Dot (matching)	Stephen's
	snaps	0			
	zippers	0			
	elastic	3"	1/4"	White	Stephen's
sketch of style here	**Fabrics**	**Quantity**	**Content**	**Describe**	**Supplier**
	base	.28 yards	100%cotton	Dots	P & B
	base				
	base				
	lining	.28	100% cotton	Stripes	P & B
Fabric Consumption: .28 yds. base .28 yds. lining	lining				

COLOR CHART

Style#	Body Color	Trim Color	Lining Color	Other	Button Color	Zipper Color	Label ID	Other
10	Dot		Stripe		Dot		Cozy Top	
10	Spring Fever		Dot		Dot		Cozy Top	
10	White		White		Black		Cozy Top	logo embroidery
10	Black		Black		White		Cozy Top	logo embroidery
10	Stripe		Spring Fever		Dot		Cozy Top	

Fabric and Trim Swatches Attach in Space Below

Fabric/Trim Spec Sheet

SWATCHES

Date: _August 15, 2020_

Vendor Name/Phone/Fax: _A & B fabrics_

1180 Town Rd., Any Town, CA 00000-0000

Phone: 000-000-0000   Fax: 000-000-0000

Fabric/Trim Name: _Juvenile Prints_

Fiber Content: _100% Cotton_

Fabric/Trim Price: _$4.50/yard_ **Fabric Width:** _45"_

Color Names/Numbers: _100 Spring Fever, 130 Dots, 150 Stripes_

Lead Times/Minimum Orders: _20 yard minimum per print;_

2 weeks when in stock, 4 - 6 weeks when reprinting

Fabric/Trim Care: _Machine wash gentle cycle, tumble-dry low._

Other Notes: _Have matching solids to go with prints._

Income Statement — Year 1

	JUL	AUG	SEP	OCT	NOV	DEC	TOTAL
INCOME							
Sales							
Freight							
Other							
Total Income							
COST OF GOODS							
Material	1200				4000		**5200**
Trims	200				1200		**1400**
Labor	600				8000		**8600**
Patterns	2400				1200		**3600**
Other							
Total COG	**4400**				**14400**		**18800**
GROSS PROFIT	**(4400)**				**(14400)**		**(18800)**
EXPENSES							
Advertising							
Bank Charges							
Car Expenses	200	200	800	800	200	200	**2400**
Dues							
Education							
Equipment Rental							
Entertainment							
Legal/Professional							
Office Supplies	400	100	100	100	100	100	**900**
Permits/Licenses	1600						**1600**
Printing			300	300			**600**
Postage			100	100	100	100	**400**
Photography			200	200			**400**
Publications							
Rent							
Shipping							
Storage							
Telephone	200	200	200	200	200	200	**1200**
Trade Shows							
Utilities							
Total Expenses	**2400**	**500**	**1700**	**1700**	**600**	**600**	**7500**
NET INCOME	**(6800)**	**(7300)**	**(9000)**	**(10700)**	**(25700)**	**(26300)**	**(26300)**

Income Statement — Year 2

	JAN	FEB	MAR	APR	MAY	JUN
INCOME						
Sales		8000	10000	2000		
Freight		200	300	100		
Other						
Total Income		**8200**	**10300**	**2100**		
COST OF GOODS						
Material	1400				4000	
Trims	200				1200	
Labor	800				8000	
Patterns	800				1200	
Other						
Total COG	**3200**				**14400**	
GROSS PROFIT	**(3200)**	**8200**	**10300**	**2100**	**(14400)**	
EXPENSES						
Advertising						
Bank Charges						
Car Expenses	200	200	800	800	200	200
Dues						
Education						
Equipment Rental						
Entertainment						
Legal/Professional				600		
Office Supplies	100	100	100	100	100	100
Permits/Licenses						
Printing			300	300		
Postage	100	100	100	100	100	100
Photography			200	200		
Publications						
Rent						
Shipping	200	300	100			100
Storage						
Telephone	300	300	300	300	300	300
Trade Shows						
Utilities						
Total Expenses	**900**	**1000**	**1900**	**2400**	**700**	**800**
NET INCOME	**(4100)**	**3100**	**11500**	**11200**	**(3900)**	**(4700)**

Income Statement—Year 2, continued

	JUL	AUG	SEP	OCT	NOV	DEC	TOTAL
INCOME							
Sales	2000	10000	10000				42000
Freight	100	300	300				1300
Other							
Total Income	2100	10300	10300				43300
COST OF GOODS							
Material			2000		10000	10000	27400
Trims			200		600	600	2800
Labor			600		20000	20000	49400
Patterns			1200		1400	1400	6000
Other							
Total COG			4000		32000	32000	85600
GROSS PROFIT	2100	10300	6300		(32000)	(32000)	(42300)
EXPENSES							
Advertising			1200	1200			2400
Bank Charges							
Car Expenses	200	200	800	800	200	200	4800
Dues							
Education							
Equipment Rental							
Entertainment			400	400			800
Legal/Professional							600
Office Supplies	100	100	100	100	100	100	1200
Permits/Licenses	800						800
Printing			600	600			1800
Postage	120	120	120	120	120	120	1320
Photography			50	50			800
Publications							
Rent							
Shipping	300	300					1300
Storage							
Telephone	400	400	400	400	400	400	4200
Trade Shows			16000				16000
Utilities							
Total Expenses	1920	1120	19820	3820	820	820	36020
NET INCOME	(4520)	4660	(8860)	(12680)	(45500)	(78320)	(78320)

Income Statement — Year 3

	JAN	FEB	MAR	APR	MAY	JUN
INCOME						
Sales		48000	60000	12000		
Freight		1200	1800	600		
Other						
Total Income		49200	61800	12600		
COST OF GOODS						
Material	2000				12000	12000
Trims	600				3600	3600
Labor	1600				24000	24000
Patterns	1600				2000	2000
Other						
Total COG	5800				41600	41600
GROSS PROFIT	(5800)	49200	61800	12600	(41600)	(41600)
EXPENSES						
Advertising	1200	1200				
Bank Charges						
Car Expenses	400	400	1200	1200	400	400
Dues						
Education						
Equipment Rental						
Entertainment						
Legal/Professional				600		
Office Supplies	200	200	200	200	200	200
Permits/Licenses						
Printing			600	600		
Postage	200	200	200	200	200	200
Photography			400	400		
Publications						
Rent						
Shipping						
Storage						500
Telephone	400	400	400	400	400	400
Trade Shows			16000			
Utilities						
Total Expenses	2400	2400	19000	3600	1200	1700
NET INCOME	(8200)	38600	81400	90400	47600	4300

Income Statement—Year 3, continued

	JUL	AUG	SEP	OCT	NOV	DEC	TOTAL
INCOME							
Sales	20000	60000	60000	20000	16000	8000	**304000**
Freight	500	1500	1500	500	400	200	**8200**
Other							
Total Income	**20500**	**61500**	**61500**	**20500**	**16400**	**8200**	**312200**
COST OF GOODS							
Material					18000	18000	**62000**
Trims					600	600	**9000**
Labor					20000	20000	**89600**
Patterns					1400	1400	**8400**
Other							
Total COG					**40000**	**40000**	**169000**
GROSS PROFIT	**20500**	**61500**	**61500**	**21500**	**(23600)**	**(31800)**	**143200**
EXPENSES							
Advertising			2000	2000			**6400**
Bank Charges							
Car Expenses	400	400	1200	1200	400	400	**8000**
Dues							
Education							
Equipment Rental							
Entertainment							
Legal/Professional							**600**
Office Supplies	200	200	200	200	200	200	**2400**
Permits/Licenses							
Printing				800	800		**2800**
Postage	200	200	200	200	200	200	**2400**
Photography				400	400		**1600**
Publications							
Rent							
Shipping	1500	1500	500	400	200	1200	**5800**
Storage							
Telephone	400	400	400	400	400	400	**4800**
Trade Shows			20000				**36000**
Utilities							
Total Expenses	**2700**	**2700**	**24500**	**5600**	**2600**	**2400**	**70800**
NET INCOME	**22100**	**80900**	**117900**	**132800**	**106600**	**72400**	**72400**

Resume

Lee Levin
1000 Main Street
Any Town, CA 00000-0000
800-000-0000
Llevin@website.com

GOAL: To turn my passion for designing unique products into a profitable business.

2015 to Present	ADORABLE KIDS, CHILDREN'S CLOTHING MANUFACTURER Assistant Designer •Developed merchandising plan with head designer. •Worked with fabric and trim manufacturers each season. •Sketched line sheets each season. •Directed sample sewers and approved all prototypes.
2013 to 2015	HENRY'S HAT AND HEADGEAR Sales Associate •Worked with owner on buy plan for the store. •Monitored all orders with vendors and sales reps. •Key sales associate in the store.
2011 to 2015	LEE'S SEWING SERVICE Principal •Designed and sewed one-of-a-kind products. •Estimated/bought fabrics and trims.
2009 to 2012	MACY'S DEPARTMENT STORE Sales Associate and Advisory Board •Represented Any Town/State on College Advisory Board. •Worked in menswear, juniors and children's departments. •Achieved highest store sales quotas in 2010.
Education	Bachelor of Science (Textiles and Business), My Town University, 2009. AA Degree (Fashion Design), Any Town Community College, 2007.
Talents	Highly motivated self-starter, meticulous seamstress, trained flat-sketch artist and excellent communicator. Fluent Spanish.
Recommendations:	Available upon request.

INDEX

CONTACT INFORMATION

GarmentoSpeak® provides publications and consulting services for manufacturers of apparel and sewn products.

Consulting

Informative Ninety-Minute Consultation: This is our most requested service for start-up companies, product development and assessing and beginning to address the needs of established and new companies. We can do this in person, by phone, fax, e-mail and regular mail. Subsequent time for additional services can be arranged. Phone Toll Free 877-823-4001 to set up an appointment.

Phone:	650-577-8215
Fax:	650-571-8483
Mail:	GarmentoSpeak
	500 Botany Court
	Foster City, CA 94404-3703
E-mail:	connieu@garmentospeak.com
Web:	www.garmentospeak.com

Publications

Cover Yourself: Adventures in the Rag Trade from Start-Ups to Stars—An adventurous ride through the rag business with a cast of characters that includes the famous, the determined and the lucky. These American's true stories are slices of life in the rag trade—where they get the goods from idea to hanger. It is the place where your clothes come to life. $14.95

Made In America: The Business of Apparel and Sewn Products Manufacturing, Third Edition $29.95

Phone:	707-823-4001
Fax:	707-823-5772
Mail:	GarmentoSpeak
	1380 Tilton Road
	Sebastopol, CA 95472-9110
E-mail:	spg@garmentospeak.com
Web:	www.garmentospeak.com